LEITH'S
HEALTHY
EATING

LEITH'S HEALTHY EATING

PUFF FAIRCLOUGH, ANNE HEUGHAN & CAROLINE WALDEGRAVE

PHOTOGRAPHS BY GRAHAM KIRK

BLOOMSBURY

First published in Great Britain in 1996
Bloomsbury Publishing Plc, 2 Soho Square, London W1V 6HB

Copyright © 1997 Leith's School of Food and Wine

The moral right of the authors has been asserted

A CIP catalogue record for this book is available from the British Library

ISBN 0 7475 2849 9

10 9 8 7 6 5 4 3 2 1

Photographer: Graham Kirk
Assisted by: David Barrett
Stylist: Helen Payne
Home Economists: Puff Fairclough
Assisted by: Staff and students at Leith's School of Food and Wine
Line drawings by: Kate Simunek

Typeset by Hewer Text Composition Services, Edinburgh
Printed by The Bath Press

CONTENTS

ACKNOWLEDGEMENTS

Teachers, students and colleagues have all helped with the making for this book. The teachers tested and gave helpful advice on many of the recipes. Many students assisted at the photography shoots with newly acquired expertise. We are very grateful to Eithne Swan for buying most of the food for testing and photography, and to Janey Orr and Kim Anderson for extra recipe ideas, and Charlie Cotton for checking the wine suggestions.

Special thanks to C.J. Jackson for her most generous loan of a laptop and her patient instructions to the novice operator, and also for the information on pasta. Thank you also to Maureen Flynn for typing some of the recipes quickly and efficiently.

Many thanks to Wendy Doyle at the Institute of Brain Chemistry and Human Nutrition, who expertly evaluated all the nutritional analysis of each recipe with great speed over a holiday.

We are very grateful to Trish Burgess who edited the script calmly, thoroughly and patiently.

Finally we would like to thank Graham Kirk, the photographer, and his team of Helen Payne and David Barrett, for all their insight and artistry and for their kindness to the students who came to assist.

INTRODUCTION

INTRODUCTION

by Anne Heughan, S.R.D.

Food and health have never been so topical, with almost every newspaper and magazine advising us what to eat and drink. Given the diversity of opinion, you could easily be forgiven for thinking that scientists never agree with one another about what constitutes a healthy diet, but in reality there has never been so much agreement.

As a result of scientific consensus, the Government has set intake targets for many of the major nutrients, but there are still plenty of issues for scientists to resolve. These extra pieces of information will be like adding the final pieces to a jigsaw but they are unlikely to change dramatically our views about the types of food we should eat. For instance, scientists no longer just see vitamins and minerals in terms of avoiding deficiency diseases, but are largely concerned with establishing the levels we need for optimal health. This may help not only to prevent chronic diseases, but also to maintain the quality of life into old age.

MODERN DISEASES

We no longer need to worry about diseases that result from undernutrition, such as rickets and scurvy, which were a major public health problem only 50 years ago. Today our problems are more likely to stem from overnutrition resulting in chronic conditions, such as coronary heart disease, certain cancers and diabetes. Of these three, coronary heart disease is the most common, and the UK has one of the highest rates in the world. While it is hard to predict exactly who will fall prey to it, we know that one in three men and one in four women currently suffer, so we all need to be concerned about it.

Many illnesses, including coronary heart disease and certain cancers, are a cumulation of several risk factors, only one of which is diet. The more risk factors you have, the greater your chance of developing the disease, but some of the risk factors are harder to change than others: for example, you cannot alter your family history, your age or your sex (men are more at risk than women). Among those you can change are smoking, high blood cholesterol and raised blood pressure, the last two being influenced by an unbalanced diet, lack of physical activity, obesity and stress.

Why do British people have a higher incidence of heart disease than the rest of Europe? It could be due to a number of factors. Those in Mediterranean countries eat about double the amount of fruit and vegetables consumed by the average British person, they eat less saturated fat and they generally take more physical activity as part of everyday life.

CAUSES OF HEART DISEASE

Coronary heart disease often begins with narrowing of the arteries that lead to the heart. This narrowing is usually caused by atherosclerosis, a build-up of fatty deposits in the arteries, which restricts the flow of blood to the heart. A heart attack occurs when the supply of blood to part of the heart is completely blocked. A blockage can also be caused by a blood clot, known as a coronary thrombosis, or a combination of atherosclerosis and a clot. To date, relatively little is known about how diet influences the thrombogenic risk factors, but research is likely to reveal more in the next few years.

What causes narrowing of the arteries? The evidence seems to point largely to our blood cholesterol levels. Blood cholesterol is a soft, waxy substance that is made in the liver and carried in the bloodstream. It is used for a variety of body functions, such as the production of hormones and proper cell function, and is not harmful in itself in the right amount. Usually, the body maintains a healthy balance of blood cholesterol, making more as necessary and getting rid of any excess. Sometimes, however, the balance goes wrong. This is when blood cholesterol

and other substances tend to narrow or 'fur-up' the artery walls. Thus, the higher the level of cholesterol in the blood, the greater the risk of developing coronary heart disease.

TYPES OF CHOLESTEROL

There are three main types of blood cholesterol: low density lipoprotein (LDL), very low density lipoprotein (VLDL) and high density lipoprotein (HDL). Each of these influences your risk of heart disease in a different way. For instance, having high levels of LDL and VLDL are thought to increase the risk of heart disease, whereas having a high level of HDL is thought to be beneficial and reduce the risk of heart disease. You can avoid high LDL by reducing your intake of saturated (animal) fat, which causes the body to make more cholesterol than it needs. High levels of HDL, on the other hand, can be encouraged by taking exercise and a moderate amount of alcohol.

While it is not unusual to see newspaper reports claiming that certain foods, such as garlic, soyabeans, oranges and wine, will help prevent heart disease, it is best to take them with a pinch of salt. No such 'magical foods' exist; overall diet and lifestyle are far more important in maintaining a healthy heart.

BASIC RULES FOR HEALTHY EATING
- *Eat plenty of fruit and vegetables – at least five portions every day.*
- *Eat more foods rich in complex carbohydrates, particularly bread, rice and pasta.*
- *Eat less fat, particularly saturated (animal) fat.*
- *Reduce your intake of salt and added sugar.*
- *Maintain your ideal body weight.*

ESSENTIAL ANTIOXIDANTS

Fruit and vegetables are rich in vitamins and minerals, particularly the antioxidant vitamins C and E, the carotenoids and other non-nutrients such as lycopene (found in tomatoes). No one is yet sure which of these antioxidant chemicals exerts the most protection against such things as coronary heart disease, but it is known that they do so by controlling unwanted free radicals. These are highly reactive molecules that occur naturally in the body, but the amount is increased, for instance, if you smoke or inhale car fumes. The body has a natural defence mechanism against the damaging effects of free radicals, in the form of antioxidant chemicals. However, if the defence mechanism slips out of balance, it is thought that free radicals may initiate heart disease or cancer by causing cell and tissue damage.

Data currently suggests that we need

IS VEGETARIANISM HEALTHY?
Current evidence seems to indicate that vegetarians are healthier than meat-eaters as they suffer less from cancer and coronary heart disease. But the reason they are healthier is not just because of the food they eat: they also tend not to smoke and to drink less alcohol.

The vegetarian diet has the potential to contain lots of fruit, vegetables and starchy carbohydrate foods. However, vegetarians need to be careful about the amount of fat in their diet as they tend to rely on cheese as a major source of protein. Ideally, this should be replaced by beans and pulses or low-fat versions of cheese, milk and yoghurt. Choosing low-fat dairy foods will not only reduce their overall fat intake, but will also help maintain their intake of calcium.

One of the commonest nutritional deficiencies among teenage girls, both vegetarian and non-vegetarian, is calcium. As bones continue to grow until the early thirties, it is essential to eat enough calcium (and take enough exercise) during these formative years.

much higher intakes of antioxidant chemicals to help prevent disease than to avoid deficiency disease. The challenge will be whether these requirements can be met from food or whether supplements or fortification of food will be required. At the moment, scientists are uncertain, so they recommend eating at least five portions of fruit and vegetables a day and reducing 'unnecessary' food intake to ensure optimum levels of antioxidants in the body.

CARBOHYDRATES

Carbohydrates are usually divided into two groups. 'Simple carbohydrates' is the term used to describe sugars, such as honey, fructose, sucrose and glucose; 'complex carbohydrates' is the term used to describe starchy, high-fibre foods which are usually plant-based in origin. Most complex carbohydrates are low in fat and contain plenty of vitamins, minerals and dietary fibre. Over the last decade our consumption of complex carbohydrates (and the amount of total energy consumed) has declined. In fact, some experts are now saying that if we increased our energy expenditure by taking more physical activity, and ate more foods rich in complex carbohydrates, such as fruit and vegetables, cereals (particularly the whole grain varieties), beans and pulses, there would be less need to cut the amount of fat we eat.

Studies confirm that where intake of complex carbohydrates is high and intake of fat is low, there is less risk of coronary heart disease. The exact role of complex carbohydrates is hard to isolate; the reduced rate of heart disease may be due to their fibre, vitamin or mineral content, or a mixture of all three. However, evidence shows that soluble fibre, which is found in beans and other pulses, oats, fruit and green leafy vegetables, can help to reduce blood cholesterol levels.

Is bran good for you?

During the 1980s, bran (the outer layer of grain) became almost synonymous with high-fibre diets. Scientific evidence showed that it helps the gut work more efficiently by making the stool softer and bulkier. However, raw wheat bran also contains a substance known as phytate, which reduces the absorption of certain minerals such as calcium, iron and zinc. Although this is not a problem in the majority of individuals, it has become increasingly recognized that bran is not in itself a prescription for good health.

It remains as true today as it did in the 1980s that we do not eat enough dietary fibre, but it is much better to eat a diet that contains plenty of fruit, vegetables and wholegrain foods, such as brown rice, wholemeal bread and pasta, than to sprinkle bran on everything. However, starting the day with a wheat bran or oat bran breakfast cereal is a positive step towards eating a high-fibre, low-fat diet.

FATS

Much of the debate on diet and health seems to focus on fat. That is because many of us eat too much fat and, in particular, too much saturated (animal) fat. Ideally, about a third of our total calories should come from fat (that is approximately 80 grams per day for the average man or woman), and no more than a tenth of our calories should come from saturated fat (approximately 25 grams per day for the average man or woman). Currently, 40 per cent of our total calories comes from fat, of which 16 per cent are from saturated fat.

Major sources of fat and saturated fat in the diet

Food	Fat%	Saturated fat%
Cakes, biscuits, etc.	19	18
Milk and milk products	19	26
Fat spreads	16	17
Meat and meat products	27	25
Snacks, confectionery	11	10
Other sources	8	4

Source: *The Dietary and Nutritional Survey of British Adults*, OPCS Social Survey Division MAFF/DOH, HMSO, London, 1991.

WHY EAT FAT?

A certain amount of body fat is required to cushion vital organs, such as the kidneys, and to help keep the body warm. Fat also helps us to absorb fat-soluble vitamins such as A, D, E and K. In addition, fat contributes towards the taste of our food. Certain fats – the polyunsaturated group – are 'essential' to health because they cannot be made by the body and are a vital component of all cell structures.

Not all fats contribute to coronary heart disease. Generally, it is saturated and trans fats (see opposite) that, if eaten in excess, will raise blood cholesterol levels.

FATTY ACIDS

Most foods are made up of the three main groups of fatty acid: saturates, monounsaturates and polyunsaturates. The last two groups can be further divided into cis or trans forms. Generally, one group of fatty acids, dominates more than another in a food or recipe. For instance, saturated fats predominate in hard cheese such as Cheddar or Red Leicester. They contain 34 grams of fat per 100 grams of cheese, of which 21 grams is saturated fat, 10 grams is monounsaturated fat, followed by 3 grams of trans fat and 1 gram of polyunsaturated fat.

As a general rule, saturated fats are found in animal foods, such as meat and dairy products, and in cakes, biscuits and pastries (see table, left). Trans fats, which account for a very small part of our diet (about 2% of energy), are created in two ways: one is in the stomach of ruminant animals, such as cows or sheep, and the other is through hydrogenating (adding hydrogen to) edible oils. Trans fatty acids are found in dairy foods, such as butter, milk and meat, and in cakes, biscuits and pastries. Recent scientific evidence suggests that trans fatty acids also raise blood cholesterol levels, so government reports recommend that we should consider reducing our intake of them. As a result many manufacturers are now producing margarines and fat spreads with very low levels of trans (and saturated) fatty acids.

The cis form of unsaturated fats has a rather different effect on blood cholesterol levels and hence on our risk of heart disease. Neither monounsaturated nor polyunsaturated fat seems to increase blood cholesterol levels, so both can be included in a healthy diet.

Polyunsaturated fat can be divided into two groups: the omega-6 polyunsaturated fats and the omega-3 polyunsaturated fats. The first group is most common in the UK and actively helps to lower blood cholesterol levels. Omega-6 fats are found in the seeds, nuts and oils from sunflowers, soya and corn. Generally, most people have enough of these fats in their diet, so they should maintain their current intake, but cut down on their total fat intake.

The omega-3 polyunsaturated fats, commonly found in oily fish, do not lower blood cholesterol levels but they help to make the blood less sticky and therefore less likely to form clots which could block an artery. On present evidence, experts do not recommend that we take fish oil supplements, but that we double our intake of oily fish, such as mackerel, herring, salmon and sardines. White fish does not contain large quantities of omega-3 fats, but it is very low in saturated fat, so is useful to include in our diet.

Meat: good or bad?

There is no need to become a vegetarian in order to be healthy. The idea that red meat is unhealthy seems to have developed for a variety of reasons; first, because meat and meat products were seen as being high in fat; second, to counterbalance the high-protein diet of the 1960s, which recommended eating plenty of steak; and third, because of concerns about animal welfare.

The truth lies somewhere in between. Meat is often no higher in fat than many other foods (see below). We certainly do not need to avoid meat, either white or red, from a nutritional point of view, but we should make sure that we also eat plenty of starchy foods, such as bread and pasta, and lots of fruit and vegetables.

Food (per portion)	Fat content (grams)
Oven chips, 125g	5.3
Cheddar cheese, 50g	16.0
Iced sponge cake, 90g	27.5
Half-fat cheese, 50g	8.0
Ice-cream, 75g	6.5
Quarter-pound hamburger, 100g	21.6
Regular crisps, 28g packet	10.5
Low-fat crisps, 28g packet	6.0
Pork pie, 125g	33.8
Fried fish, 175g	18.0
Boiled gammon, lean, 100g	5.5
Roast pork, lean, 100g	6.9
Roast chicken, lean, 100g	5.4
Roast leg of lamb, 100g	8.1
Steak, grilled, 150g	9.0

Source: *The Composition of Foods* by R.A. McCance and E.M. Widdowson, Fifth Edition, Royal Society of Chemistry and MAFF, London, 1994.

SOURCES OF FAT

SATURATED FAT

Fatty meats (sausages, hamburgers), high-fat dairy foods (cream, butter, hard cheeses, full-fat milk), cakes, biscuits, pies, snacks, hard margarine, lard, beef dripping, ghee, coconut and coconut oil.

MONOUNSATURATED FAT

Peanuts and peanut oil, avocados, hazelnuts and hazelnut oil, rapeseed oil, olives and olive oil, most soft margarines.

POLYUNSATURATED FAT (OMEGA-6s)

Sunflower seeds and oil, soya oil, corn oil, sesame seeds and oil, polyunsaturated margarines, walnuts and walnut oil, almonds, brazil nuts.

POLYUNSATURATED FAT (OMEGA-3s)

Oily fish, such as mackerel, salmon, herring, sardines, kippers, rapeseed oil and many green leafy vegetables.

REDUCING FAT AND SATURATED FAT INTAKE

- *Use less oil in cooking, particularly when browning meat or onions. Use an unsaturated oil, such as sunflower, olive, rapeseed or soya oil, in a non-stick frying pan.*
- *Use low-fat dairy foods, such as skimmed or semi-skimmed milk, low-fat yoghurt and low-fat cheese. Coffee whiteners are not an ideal substitute for milk as they are usually high in saturated fat and sodium and low in calcium.*
- *Choose a polyunsaturated margarine or a reduced-fat or low-fat spread instead of butter or hard margarine. A polyunsaturated margarine will always be labelled 'high in polyunsaturates'.*
- *Make your own salad dressing as it is possible to use less oil to vinegar. Alternatively, choose a reduced-fat mayonnaise and a fat-free salad dressing.*
- *Don't add extra butter or other fat to vegetables.*
- *Use low-fat yoghurt, low-fat fromage frais or low-fat ice-cream instead of cream.*
- *Choose extra lean cuts of meat, such as beef, pork, veal or game, and remember to trim off any excess fat.*
- *Choose chicken and turkey as they are low in fat once the skin is removed.*
- *Choose fish (both white and oily) more often.*
- *Use less meat by including beans and vegetables in casseroles, stews or stir-fries.*
- *Eat fewer high-fat snacks, such as cakes, biscuits, chocolate and crisps. If you need something between meals, replace your usual snacks with bread, fruit or unbuttered bread-type buns and scones.*
- *Have jacket potatoes (without any extra fat) instead of chips.*
- *Choose reduced-fat versions of foods such as crisps and sausages.*

- *Use potato topping (without additional fat or eggs) instead of pastry for savoury dishes.*
- *Grill, bake, steam or microwave foods whenever possible; if you need to fry, reduce the amount and type of oil you use.*
- *Choose vegetable-based sauces for pasta rather than creamy ones.*
- *Cut down on chips, and if you do cook them, cut them thick and straight and fry in an oil that is high in polyunsaturates. Change the oil frequently.*

DIETARY CHOLESTEROL

Despite numerous myths to the contrary, dietary cholesterol is not the major culprit in causing heart disease. This myth persists because many foods that are high in dietary cholesterol, such as meat products and dairy foods, are also high in saturated fat, thus making it difficult for researchers to sort out which has the most powerful effect on blood cholesterol levels. Even so, it is unwise to eat large quantities of cholesterol-rich food.

Some people are more sensitive to dietary cholesterol than others. For example, those with a family history of high blood cholesterol are usually advised to eat less dietary cholesterol (as well as less saturated fat). This means cutting down on offal, egg yolks and shellfish, particularly prawns, crab and lobster, as they are higher in dietary cholesterol than mussels, scallops, oysters and clams.

Full-fat milk for children?

Milk consumption has declined since 1980 because many people believe it is high in fat. While full-fat milk can certainly make a significant contribution to our fat intake, it also provides valuable nutrients such as protein and calcium. The answer to this dilemma lies with low-fat milks (skimmed or semi-skimmed). Both provide the same amount of calcium, protein and B vitamins as full-fat milk, but fewer calories and less fat. A glass of full-fat milk contains 6 grams of fat, whereas a glass of semi-skimmed milk contains only 2.5 grams of fat. Although low-fat milks provide less vitamin A, milk is not an important source of it, so the shortfall can be easily made up from other sources. The conclusion, then, is that if your children are over five and eating well, do encourage them to have low-fat milks in preference to full-fat milk. The advice between the ages of two and five is less clear cut. It really depends on whether your children are eating and growing well. If they are, they can certainly drink semi-skimmed milk. More important, though, is to establish good eating habits rather than to worry about the type of milk they drink.

SALT

Salt is the name of a compound, sodium chloride, that occurs naturally in our food. It consists of approximately 40 per cent sodium and 60 per cent chloride. The preservative properties of salt have been known of for thousands of years, but the sodium in it also plays an important role in controlling the body's fluid balance.

We eat far too much salt, approximately 12 grams or just over 2 teaspoons a day, which is well in excess of our bodies' requirements of 4 grams or less a day. Consuming too much salt may lead to high blood pressure in some people, which in turn can cause heart disease and strokes. It is therefore recommended that we cut down on salt consumption. All the salt we need can be found naturally in fruit, vegetables, meat, fish and cereals.

About three-quarters of our salt intake comes from processed foods, particularly ham, bacon, sausages, canned and packet soups, soy sauce, cheese, crisps, salted nuts and smoked fish. The rest of the salt in our diet is added during cooking or at the table. While the recipes in this book include salt, we do encourage you to start reducing the amount you add to food over the coming months. Try to cut down gradually so that your taste buds adapt more easily; it can take a couple of months to get used to eating less salt. To help compensate for its loss, increase your intake of herbs and spices rather than salt substitutes because these still contain salt and will not help you to lose your taste for it.

SUGARS

Despite their bad press, refined carbohydrates, such as sugar and sugary foods, have not been linked directly with causing coronary heart disease, high blood pressure or diabetes. However, the frequent consumption of sugar and sugary foods and drinks can increase the chance of dental caries and of becoming overweight. There is a whole host of sugars that you need to watch out for on the food labels; syrup, honey, raw sugar cane, dextrose, corn syrup, glucose, fructose and, of course, brown and white sugar. These sugars contain no vitamins or minerals in significant amounts – only calories. In fact, a teaspoon of sugar is approximately 20 calories.

Many children and adults eat far too many sugary foods, such as cakes, biscuits and chocolate, so they should reduce their intake of these foods.

MAINTAINING BODY WEIGHT

As a nation, the British are getting fatter. In 1987 approximately 9 per cent of us were obese. The level has now increased to 14 per cent. Maintaining ideal body weight is important, as overweight people are more at risk from cancer, diabetes and coronary heart disease. However, don't be too complacent if you are thin or lean: you still need to consider what you eat.

Losing weight is not just about dieting. It should be about re-educating your eating habits and taking more physical activity. This does not mean you have to join the local gym, but it does mean doing more walking or cycling, for example. Fat is certainly the most calorific of all foods, providing 9 calories per gram, whereas protein and carbohydrate provide only 4 calories per gram. Alcohol is also calorific, providing 7 calories per gram. So forget the old-fashioned notion that bread and potatoes are fattening and start tucking in (but without smothering them in fat).

Certain diets claim to work by such means as not combining protein and carbohydrate at the same meal, or by claiming that a grapefruit eaten before each meal will burn up the fat. The real reason those diets work, however, is because most of them limit the amount of food (calories) you eat. The simple rules for a successful reducing diet are to choose foods low in fat, to reduce the amount you eat and to change your pattern of eating. You also need to think long-term, because weight loss is slow after the first week, usually in the region of 225–675 grams (½–1½lb) a week. A recent two-year research project showed that overweight people lost more weight on a high-carbohydrate and low-fat diet than by calorie counting.

Exercise is the second most important aspect of a reducing diet, but it does not burn up as many calories as you might think. None the less, it is excellent for general well-being and helps tone up the muscles, including the heart. While it is not a cure for obesity, it certainly helps those who are slightly overweight to lose a few pounds.

Additives
People generally exaggerate the risks attached to food additives. For most of us the risk from eating food additives is far less than from eating, say, too much saturated fat. Many additives prolong the life of food, making it safer to eat. They can also stop the growth of bacteria and moulds, and improve the taste, texture and even nutritional value of our food. Without them, the variety of foods we can eat would be much reduced. However, a few individuals do show adverse reactions to certain additives, such as tartrazine and benzoic acid, so those with sensitivities should try to avoid these additives.

ALCOHOL

Stimulant, tranquillizer, anaesthetic, medicine and food – alcohol is one of the oldest and most widely used drugs. While it can be toxic in large quantities, it is socially acceptable in moderation.

BENEFITS OF ALCOHOL

Many studies have shown that moderate drinkers have a lower risk of coronary heart disease than non-drinkers or heavy drinkers. However, re-analysis of these studies, putting those who have never drunk in the non-drinking group rather than those who have abstained from drinking for a variety of reasons, some medical, has yielded different results. While there is no conclusive evidence that moderate drinking is good for the heart, it is also true to say that it isn't harmful.

Some studies have shown that red wine is better for us than white wine. This is because red wine contains more phenols, which act as antioxidants (see page 5). However, these studies have been criticized because the red wine drinkers also consumed more fruit and vegetables.

DISADVANTAGES OF ALCOHOL

Alcohol interferes with the absorption of certain nutrients, namely folic acid and vitamin B12, which the liver requires to break down the alcohol so that it can be used as energy. In addition, alcohol is a diuretic (causes increased urination) and can therefore cause loss of water-soluble minerals such as potassium and magnesium.

Excessive amounts of alcohol can cause raised blood pressure, cirrhosis of the liver and brain damage. As alcohol tends to be low in nutrients but high in calories, increased consumption can also lead to weight problems.

This apparently conflicting information on alcohol does not mean you have to be teetotal or, on the other hand, take up drinking. But you should stick to the present recommended limits (see below) of no more than four units a day for men and no more than three units a day for women, with at least a couple of days a week without alcohol. Note that you are strongly advised not to drink alcohol during pregnancy or in the six months before conception.

One Unit of Alcohol Equals
- *1 glass, 125ml/4fl oz wine (8–9% volume)*
- *290ml/½ pint ordinary beer, lager or cider*
- *150ml/¼ pint strong beer, lager or cider*
- *1 small glass, 80ml/2¼fl oz sherry, port or Madeira*
- *1 pub measure, 24ml/¼ gill* spirits, such as gin or whisky*
- *2 glasses, 250ml/8fl oz low-alcohol (3% volume) wine*

*A Scottish pub measure of spirits is 1.2 units of alcohol.

COFFEE

There has been much research to investigate whether coffee, with or without caffeine, fresh or instant, is bad for your heart. So far the evidence seems to suggest that the method of making coffee is far more important than the type you drink. Boiled or percolated ground coffee, drunk strong and black, seems to raise blood cholesterol levels. The majority of British people drink coffee which is filtered, instant or cafetière-style, so we should not be affected.

The caffeine found in tea and coffee is a stimulant which can cause irritability, sleeplessness and increased blood pressure, although only temporarily. If you are drinking a lot of coffee or tea and you suffer any of these symptoms, you should consider cutting down.

GARLIC

The garlic clove, along with olive oil

and red wine, symbolizes the Mediterranean diet on which so much praise has been heaped in recent years. So just how justified is this praise?

Extensive research on garlic shows that its chemical components make the blood less sticky and therefore less liable to clot. However, it seems to be effective at reducing heart disease only in those who have already had a heart attack. Current evidence does not seem to justify taking garlic capsules or tablets to maintain a healthy heart, but there is no harm taking garlic in your food.

SO WHAT DOES THIS ALL MEAN?

Eating healthily is essential for everyone, not just those who have been advised to make changes by their doctor. Many people have already altered their diet, but some are reluctant to do so on the grounds that the experts don't agree, so they might as well continue just as they are. The best plan is simply to follow the basic rules of good eating (see page 5).

Don't be disheartened if changing your eating habits means cutting out or down on your favourite foods – there are many new things to enjoy, so why not go ahead and experiment? We hope this book will give you the encouragement you need.

Consider what foods you buy and how you cook them as both can make a difference to the nutritional content of your diet. Make the changes gradually because a sudden change may result in

slipping back into old habits. You could start by changing the milk you drink or the spread you use on bread, and by trying a new sandwich or recipe once a week.

Meals and snacks should consist of plenty of bread, rice, pasta or potato, with lots of vegetables and fruit, plus fish or a small portion of meat or dairy produce. You could, for example, have boiled rice with stir-fried vegetables and pork, or a 'doorstep' sandwich filled with lots of salad and tuna, or pasta with tomato sauce and a sprinkling of Parmesan cheese, followed by fruit.

It is perfectly possible to adapt many of your family's favourite recipes so that they are lower in fat, particularly saturated fat, by using fewer and different types of fats and oils and fewer high-fat foods than suggested in the original recipe. This can also be achieved by using more beans and pulses, vegetables or fruit.

Try to cut down the amount of salt you add during cooking, except when making bread, where salt is used to control how much the dough rises. You may also wish to add a little to French dressing to prevent it tasting 'oily'. After a while your tastebuds will get used to eating less salt. In fact, you may even find that food tastes better without it.

It is easy to reduce the amount of sugar in fruit-based dishes like crumble, stewed fruit, fruit salads, fools and mousses, but it is harder to produce acceptable results in other puddings or cakes and gâteaux. Rather than do without, serve them occasionally for a special treat.

Many people believe that eating healthily means never eating chips or having a piece of chocolate cake ever again. This is simply not true. A healthy diet is all a question of balance, but it must be the right balance.

Food is one of life's great pleasures and it can continue to be pleasurable even if you change your eating habits. The recipes in this book prove over and over again that healthy eating can be every bit as delicious and satisfying as any other sort. Just try them and see.

CONVERSION TABLES

CONVERSION TABLES

The tables below are approximate, and do not conform in all respects to the conventional conversions, but we have found them convenient for cooking. Use either metric or imperial measurements: do not mix the two.

Weight

Imperial	Metric	Imperial	Metric
¼oz	7–8g	½oz	15g
¾oz	20g	1oz	30g
2oz	55g	3oz	85g
4oz (¼lb)	110g	5oz	140g
6oz	170g	7oz	200g
8oz (½lb)	225g	9oz	255g
10oz	285g	11oz	310g
12oz (¾lb)	340g	13oz	370g
14oz	400g	15oz	425g
16oz (1lb)	450g	1¼lb	560g
1½lb	675g	2lb	900g
3lb	1.35kg	4lb	1.8kg
5lb	2.3kg	6lb	2.7kg
7lb	3.2kg	8lb	3.6kg
9lb	4.0kg	10lb	4.5kg

Australian cup measures

	Metric	Imperial
1 cup flour	140g	5oz
1 cup sugar (crystal or caster)	225g	8oz
1 cup brown sugar, firmly packed	170g	6oz
1 cup icing sugar, sifted	170g	6oz
1 cup butter	225g	8oz
1 cup honey, golden syrup, treacle	370g	12oz
1 cup fresh breadcrumbs	55g	2oz
1 cup packaged dry breadcrumbs	140g	5oz
1 cup crushed biscuit crumbs	110g	4oz
1 cup rice, uncooked	200g	7oz
1 cup mixed fruit or individual fruit, such as sultanas	170g	6oz
1 cup nuts, chopped	110g	4oz
1 cup coconut, desiccated	85g	3oz

Approximate American/European conversions

Commodity	USA	Metric	Imperial
Flour	1 cup	140g	5oz
Caster and granulated sugar	1 cup	225g	8oz
Caster and granulated sugar	2 level tablespoons	30g	1oz
Brown sugar	1 cup	170g	6oz
Butter/margarine/lard	1 cup	225g	8oz
Sultanas/raisins	1 cup	200g	7oz
Currants	1 cup	140g	5oz
Ground almonds	1 cup	110g	4oz
Golden syrup	1 cup	340g	12oz
Uncooked rice	1 cup	200g	7oz
Grated cheese	1 cup	110g	4oz
Butter	1 stick	110g	4oz

Liquid measures

Imperial	ml	fl oz
1 teaspoon	5	
2 scant tablespoons	28	1
4 scant tablespoons	56	2
¼ pint (1 gill)	150	5
⅓ pint	190	6.6
½ pint	290	10
¾ pint	425	15
1 pint	570	20
1¾ pints	1000 (1 litre)	35

Australian

250ml	1 cup
20ml	1 tablespoon
5ml	1 teaspoon

Approximate American/European conversions

American	European
1 teaspoon	1 teaspoon/5ml
½fl oz	1 tablespoon/½fl oz/15ml
¼ cup	4 tablespoons/2fl oz/55ml
½ cup plus 2 tablespoons	¼ pint/5fl oz/150ml
1¼ cups	½ pint/10fl oz/290ml
1 pint/16fl oz	1 pint/20fl oz/570ml
2½ pints (5 cups)	1.1 litres/2 pints
10 pints	4.5 litres/8 pints

Useful measurements

Measurement	Metric	Imperial
1 American cup	225ml	8fl oz
1 egg, size 3	56ml	2fl oz
1 egg white	28ml	1fl oz
1 rounded tablespoon flour	30g	1oz
1 rounded tablespoon cornflour	30g	1oz
1 rounded tablespoon caster sugar	30g	1oz
2 rounded tablespoons fresh breadcrumbs	30g	1oz
2 level teaspoons gelatine	8g	¼oz

30g/1oz granular (packet) aspic sets
570ml/1 pint liquid.

15g/½ oz powdered gelatine, or 4 leaves, will set 570ml/1 pint liquid. (However, in hot weather, or if the liquid is very acid, like lemon juice, or if the jelly contains solid pieces of food and is to be turned out of the dish or mould, 20g/¾oz should be used.)

Wine quantities

Imperial	ml	fl oz
Average wine bottle	750	25
1 glass wine	100	3½
1 glass port or sherry	70	2
1 glass liqueur	45	1

Lengths

Imperial	Metric
½in	1cm
1in	2.5cm
2in	5cm
6in	15cm
12in	30cm

Oven temperatures

°C	°F	Gas mark	AMERICAN	AUSTRALIAN
70	150	¼	COOL	VERY SLOW
80	175	¼		
100	200	½		
110	225	½		
130	250	1	VERY SLOW	SLOW
140	275	1		
150	300	2	SLOW	
170	325	3	MODERATE	MODERATELY SLOW
180	350	4		
190	375	5	MODERATELY HOT	MODERATE
200	400	6	FAIRLY HOT	
220	425	7	HOT	MODERATELY HOT
230	450	8	VERY HOT	
240	475	8		HOT
250	500	9	EXTREMELY HOT	
270	525	9		VERY HOT
290	550	9		

FOOD SAFETY

FOOD SAFETY

These are the most important factors to take into account for food safety.

1. Bugs like warmth, moisture and to be left undisturbed, so try not to give them these ideal conditions.

2. Keep cooking utensils and hands clean. Change J-cloths, tea towels and washing-up brushes regularly.

3. Store raw meat at the bottom of the refrigerator so that any meat juices cannot drip on to cooked food.

4. Wrap food up loosely – let it breathe.

5. Don't put hot food into the refrigerator – it will raise the temperature. Refrigerators should be kept at 5°C.

6. Get food to cool down as quickly as possible.

7. Never cover cooling hot food.

8. Avoid cross-contamination of germs – store raw and cooked foods separately as far as possible. If you mix raw and cooked foods, they should both be cold and then reheated thoroughly. Avoid keeping food warm for any length of time: it should be either hot or cold.

9. Never cook large items (e.g. whole chickens) from frozen.

10. Salmonella in eggs: consumption of raw eggs or uncooked dishes made from them, such as home-made mayonnaise, mousse and ice-cream, carries the risk of food poisoning. If you do use raw eggs, make sure that you use only the freshest (pasteurized eggs are available), that the dishes are eaten as soon as possible after making and that they are never left for more than 1 hour at room temperature.

Vulnerable people such as the elderly, the sick, babies, toddlers and pregnant women should only eat eggs that have been thoroughly cooked until both white and yolk are solid.

MENU PLANNING

MENU PLANNING

The most obvious rule, but the most important, must be to **keep it simple**. There is no point in attempting so much that the quality of execution is threatened.

Don't be too proud to stick the plan of action on the wall and follow it slavishly. Professional cooks do it all the time and it saves their sanity. It also saves a lot of time.

Menu content: There are also a few mental checks that you should run through when planning a menu, as much for the gastronomic pleasure and interest of the diner as for healthy eating.

1. Avoid too many eggs in the meal.

2. Check that the vegetables are sufficiently interesting. Avoid two members of the same family (e.g. cauliflower, sprouts).

3. Check that the first or main course and the pudding are not predominantly fruit, such as melon to start, meat, poultry or fish with a fruity sauce, and fruit salad to finish.

4. Check that ingredients are not repeated.

5. Check that no two courses contain similar poultry or meat, e.g. chicken liver salad, coq au vin.

6. Check that the meal contains good colour, texture and taste contrast.

7. Check that the wines are in the right order and are suitable to accompany the food. In brief: red should follow white, older wines should follow younger ones; strong, big wines should follow delicate light ones; white wines go with fish, white meat and delicate poultry; red wines go with red meat, poultry, game and cheese.

Colour: Unless you are deliberately designing a dish or a menu to suit a colour theme, such as an all-red fruit salad, the best rule is contrast without garishness. The commonest problem is too white a meal, such as pale soup followed by chicken, cauliflower and rice.

Texture: Again, contrast is the thing. If the main course is a tender casserole served with mashed potatoes to mop up the gravy, provide something crunchy, such as crisp French beans, to go with it. Some cooks have found their food processors too seductive to resist and the result can be a smooth soup, followed by lasagne, followed by a fruit fool, so that guests long for something they can quite literally get their teeth into.

FOOD PRESENTATION

FOOD PRESENTATION

If food looks delicious, people are predisposed to think that it tastes delicious. Serving at the table can be rather fraught, and there is also the risk of the food getting cold by the time everyone is served, so it is often preferable to present individual servings which can be arranged in the kitchen and brought straight to the table.
At Leith's School we have gradually developed a set of rules which can be used as guidelines when presenting food. Fashion may dictate the method – be it stylish *nouvelle cuisine* or chunky real food – but the guidelines are the same.

1. Keep it warm
Always serve food on warm plates. Nothing destroys anticipation more than cold plates.

2. Keep it simple
Over-decorated food often looks messed about – no longer appetizing. The more cluttered the plate, the less attractive it inevitably becomes.

3. Keep it fresh
Nothing looks more off-putting than tired food. For example, salad wilts when dressed in advance.

4. Keep it relevant
A sprig of fresh watercress complements lamb cutlets nicely. The texture, taste and colour all do something for the lamb. But scratchy sprigs of parsley, though they might provide the colour, are unpleasant to eat.

5. Best side uppermost
Usually, the side of a steak or a cutlet that is grilled first looks the best, so should be placed uppermost. Bones are generally unsightly and, if they cannot be clipped off or removed, should be tucked out of the way.

6. Centre height
Dishes served on platters, such as a chicken sauté, are best given 'centre height', i.e. arranged so that the mound of food is higher in the middle with sides sloping down. Coat carefully and evenly with the sauce, if any. Do not overload serving platters with food as this makes serving difficult.

7. Overlapping
Chops, steaks and sliced meats look best evenly overlapping. This way, more of them can be fitted comfortably on the serving dish than if placed side by side.

8. Contrasting rows
Cocktail canapés look good if arranged in rows, each row consisting of one variety, rather than dotted about. Pay attention to contrasting colour.

9. Diagonal lines
Diamond shapes and diagonal lines are easier to achieve than straight ones. The eye is more conscious of unevenness in verticals, horizontals and rectangles.

10. Not too many colours
As with any design, it is easier to get a pleasing effect if the colours are controlled – say, just green and white, or just pink and green, or chocolate and coffee colours, or even two shades of one colour. Adding every available garnish to a salad tends to look garish. There are exceptions, of course: a colourful salad Niçoise can look very attractive.

11. Contrasting simple and elaborate
If the dish or bowl is elaborately decorated, contrastingly simple food tends to show it off better. A Victorian fruit épergne with ornate stem and silver carving will look stunning filled with fresh strawberries. Conversely, a plain white plate sets off pretty food design to perfection.

12. Uneven numbers
As a rule, uneven numbers of, say, portions of meat on a platter look better than even numbers. This is especially true of small numbers.

DICTIONARY OF COOKING TERMS AND KITCHEN FRENCH

DICTIONARY OF COOKING TERMS AND KITCHEN FRENCH

Bain-marie A baking tin half-filled with hot water in which terrines, custards, etc. stand while cooking. The food is protected from direct fierce heat and cooks in a gentle, steamy atmosphere. Also a large container that will hold a number of pans standing in hot water, used to keep soups, sauces, etc. hot without further cooking.

Bard To tie bacon or pork fat over a joint of meat, game bird or poultry, to be roasted. This helps to prevent the flesh from drying out.

Baste To spoon over liquid (sometimes stock, sometimes fat) during cooking to prevent drying out and to promote flavour.

Beurre noisette Browned butter; *see* Noisette.

Blanch Originally, to whiten by boiling briefly, e.g. to boil sweetbreads or brains to remove traces of blood, or to boil almonds to make the brown skin easy to remove, leaving the nuts white. Now commonly used to mean parboiling, as in blanching vegetables when they are parboiled prior to freezing, or precooked so that they have only to be reheated before serving.

Blanquette A stew made without prior frying of the meat. Usually used for lamb, chicken or veal. The sauce is often thickened with an egg and cream liaison.

Bouillon Broth or uncleared stock.

Bouquet garni Parsley stalks, small bay leaf, fresh thyme, celery stalk, sometimes with a blade of mace, tied together with string and used to flavour stews, etc. Removed before serving.

Braise To bake or stew slowly on a bed of vegetables in a covered pan.

Brunoise Vegetables cut into very small dice.

Caramel Sugar cooked to a toffee.

Chine To remove the backbone from a rack of ribs. Carving is almost impossible if the butcher has not 'chined' the meat.

Collops Small slices of meat, taken from a tender cut such as neck of lamb.

Concasser To chop roughly.

Consommé Clear soup.

Coulis Essentially a thick sauce, e.g. coulis de tomatoes, thick tomato sauce; raspberry coulis, raspberry sauce.

Court bouillon Liquid used for cooking fish.

Cream To beat ingredients together, such as butter and fat when making a sponge cake.

Croustade Bread case baked until crisp. Used to contain hot savoury mixtures for a canapé, savoury, or as a garnish.

Croûte Literally 'crust'. Sometimes a pastry case, as in fillet of beef en croûte, sometimes toasted or fried bread, as in Scotch woodcock or scrambled eggs on toast.

Croûtons Small, evenly sized cubes of fried bread used as a soup garnish and occasionally in other dishes.

Dariole Small, castle-shaped mould used for moulding rice salads and sometimes for cooking cake mixtures.

Déglacer To loosen and liquefy the fat, sediment and browned juices stuck at the bottom of a frying pan or saucepan by adding liquid (usually stock, water or wine) and stirring while boiling.

Deglaze See Déglacer.

Dégorger To extract the juices from meat, fish or vegetables, generally by salting, then soaking or washing. Usually done to remove indigestible or strong-tasting juices.

Dépouiller To skim off the scum from a sauce or stock: a splash of cold stock is added to the boiling liquid. This helps to bring scum and fat to the surface, which can then be skimmed more easily.

Dropping consistency The consistency where a mixture will drop reluctantly from a spoon, neither pouring off nor obstinately adhering.

Duxelles Finely chopped raw mushrooms, sometimes with chopped shallots or chopped ham, often used as a stuffing.

Egg wash Beaten raw egg, sometimes with salt, used for glazing bread to give it a shine when baked.

Emulsion A stable suspension of fat and other liquid, e.g. mayonnaise, hollandaise.

Entrecôte Sirloin steak.

Entrée Traditionally a dish served before the main course, but usually served as a main course today.

Entremet Dessert or sweet course, excluding pastry sweets.

Escalope A thin slice of meat, sometimes beaten out flat to make it thinner and larger.

Farce Stuffing.

Fecule Farinaceous thickening, usually arrowroot or cornflour.

Flamber To set alcohol alight. Usually to burn off the alcohol, but often simply for dramatic effect. (Past tense flambé or flambée; English: to flame.)

Flame See Flamber.

Fold To mix with a gentle lifting motion, rather than to stir vigorously. The aim is to avoid beating out air while mixing.

Frappé Iced, or set in a bed of crushed ice.

Fumet Strong-flavoured liquor used for flavouring sauces. Usually the liquid in which fish has been poached, or the liquid that has run from fish during baking. Sometimes used of meat or truffle-flavoured liquors.

Glace de viande Reduced brown stock, very strong in flavour, used for adding body and colour to sauces.

Gratiner To brown under a grill after the surface of the dish has been sprinkled with breadcrumbs. Dishes finished like this are sometimes called gratinée or au gratin.

Hors d'oeuvre Usually simply means the first course. Sometimes used to denote a variety or selection of many savoury titbits served with drinks, or a mixed first course (hors d'oeuvres variés).

Infuse To steep or heat gently to extract flavour, as when infusing milk with onion slices.

Julienne Vegetables or citrus rind cut in thin matchstick shapes or very fine shreds.

Jus or jus de viande God's gravy, i.e. juices that occur naturally in cooking, not a made-up sauce. Also juice.

Jus lié Thickened gravy.

Knock down or knock back To punch or knead out the air in risen dough so that it resumes its pre-risen bulk.

Lard To thread strips of bacon fat (or somctimes anchovy) through meat to give it flavour, and, in the case of fat, to make up any deficiency in very lean meat.

Lardons Small strips or cubes of pork fat or bacon generally used as a garnish.

Liaison Ingredients for binding together and thickening sauce, soup or other liquid, e.g. roux, bcurrc manié, egg yolk and cream, blood.

Macédoine Small diced mixed vegetables, usually containing some root vegetables. Sometimes used of fruit, meaning a fruit salad.

Macerate To soak food in a syrup or liquid to allow flavours to mix.

Mandolin Frame of metal or wood with adjustable blades set in it for finely slicing cucumbers, potatoes, etc.

Marinade The liquid described below. Usually contains oil, onion, bay leaf and vinegar or wine.

Marinate To soak meat, fish or vegetables before cooking in acidulated liquid containing flavourings and herbs. This gives flavour and tenderizes the meat.

Marmite French word for a covered earthenware soup container in which the soup is both cooked and served.

Medallions Small rounds of meat, evenly cut. Also small round biscuits. Occasionally used of vegetables if cut in flat, round discs.

Mirepoix The bed of braising vegetables described under Braise.

Mortifier To hang meat, poultry or game.

Napper To coat, mask or cover.

Needleshreds Fine, evenly cut shreds of citrus rind (French julienne) generally used as a garnish.

Noisette Literally 'nut'. Usually means nut-brown, as in beurre noisctte, i.e. butter browned over heat to a nut colour. Also hazelnut. Also boneless rack of lamb rolled and tied, cut into neat rounds.

Nouvelle cuisine Style of cooking that promotes light and delicate dishes often using unusual combinations of very fresh ingredients, attractively arranged.

Oyster Small piece of meat found on cithcr side of the backbone of a chicken. Said to be the best flavoured flesh. (Also a bivalve mollusc!)

Papillote A wrapping of paper in which fish or meat is cooked to contain the aroma and flavour. The dish is brought to the table still wrapped up. Foil is sometimes used, but as it does not puff up dramatically, it is less satisfactory.

Parboil To half-boil or partially soften by boiling.

Pass To strain or push through a sieve.

Pâté A savoury paste of liver, pork, game, etc.

Paupiette Beef (or pork or veal) olive, i.e. a thin layer of meat, spread with a soft farce, rolled up, tied with string and cooked slowly.

Piquer To insert in meats or poultry a large julienne of fat, bacon, ham, truffle, etc.

Poussin Baby chicken.

Prove To put dough or yeasted mixture to rise before baking.

Purée Liquidized, sieved or finely mashed fruit or vegetables.

Quenelles A fine minced fish or meat mixture formed into small portions and poached. Served in a sauce, or as a garnish to other dishes.

Ragout A stew.

Réchauffée A reheated dish made with previously cooked food.

Reduce To reduce the amount of liquid by rapid boiling, causing evaporation and a consequent strengthening of flavour in the remaining liquid.

Refresh To hold boiled green vegetables under a cold tap, or to dunk them immediately in cold water to prevent their cooking further in their own steam, and to set the colour.

Repere Flour mixed with water or white of egg, used to seal pans when cooking something slowly, such as lamb ragout.

Revenir To fry meat or vegetables quickly in hot fat in order to warm them through.

Roux A basic liaison or thickening for a sauce or soup. Melted butter to which flour has been added.

Rouille Garlic and oil emulsion used as flavouring.

Salamander A hot oven or grill used for browning or glazing the tops of cooked dishes, or a hot iron or poker for branding the top with lines or a criss-cross pattern.

Salmis A game stew sometimes made with cooked game, or partially roasted game.

Sauter Method of frying in a deep-frying pan or sautoir. The food is continually tossed or shaken so that it browns quickly and evenly.

Sautoir Deep-frying pan with a lid used for recipes that require fast frying and then slower cooking (with the lid on).

Scald Of milk: to heat until on the point of boiling, when some movement can be seen at the edges of the pan but there is no overall bubbling. Of muslin, cloths, etc.: to dunk in clean boiling water, generally to sterilize.

Seal or seize To brown meat rapidly, usually in fat, for flavour and colour.

Season Of food: to flavour, generally with salt and pepper. Of iron frying pans, griddles, etc.: to prepare new equipment for use generally by coating with oil and sprinkling with salt, and placing over a high heat. This prevents subsequent rusting and sticking.

Slake To mix flour, arrowroot, cornflour or custard powder to a thin paste with a small quantity of cold water.

Supreme Choice piece of poultry (usually from the breast).

Sweat To cook gently, usually in butter or oil, but sometimes in the food's own juices, without frying or browning.

Tammy A fine muslin cloth through which sauces are sometimes forced. After this treatment they look beautifully smooth and shiny.

Tammy strainer A fine mesh strainer, conical in shape, used to produce the effect described under Tammy.

Terrine Pâté or minced mixture baked or steamed in a loaf tin or earthenware container.

Timbale A dish that has been cooked in a castle-shaped mould, or a dish served piled up high.

Tournedos Fillet steak. Usually refers to a one-portion piece of grilled fillet.

To turn vegetables To shape carrots or turnips to a small barrel shape. To cut mushrooms into a decorative spiral pattern.

To turn olives To remove the olive stone with a spiral cutting movement.

Well A hollow or dip made in a pile or bowlful of flour, exposing the tabletop or the bottom of the bowl, into which other ingredients are placed prior to mixing.

Zest The thin-coloured skin of an orange or lemon, used to give flavour. It is very thinly pared without any of the bitter white pith.

METHODS OF COOKING

METHODS OF COOKING

WAYS OF COOKING MEAT

The tougher the meat, or the larger its volume, the more slowly it must be cooked. The quick methods of cooking – frying and grilling – are suitable for small pieces of tender meat, whereas the slower methods – braising, stewing, etc. – are best for the tougher cuts.

Three factors determine the toughness of a particular cut of meat: the age of the animal (the older it is, the tougher it will be); the activity of the particular joint (the neck, shoulders, chest and legs are used far more than the back of a quadruped and are therefore tougher); and finally the texture of the fibres.

Muscle tissue is made up of long thin cells or muscle fibres bound together by sheets of connective tissue. Individual fibres can be as long as the whole muscle. Bundles of fibres are organized in groups to form an individual muscle. The lengthways structure of muscles is what we call the grain of the meat. It is easier to carve and chew in the direction of the grain. That is why we cut across the grain to make for easier chewing. The connective tissue is the harness of the muscle and is seen as gristle, tendons, etc. Connective tissue is made up of three main proteins: collagen, which can be converted by long, slow cooking into gelatine; elastin, which is elastic and not changed by heat; and reticulen, which is fibrous and not changed by heat.

Tender cuts of meat, such as sirloin steak, have relatively few connective tissues and as they cook, the meat fibres shrink and lose moisture. When overcooked, the juices finally dry up and a once tender piece of meat becomes well done, tough and dry. However, a tough joint of meat, such as oxtail, which has a lot of connective tissue, can become very moist during cooking. The collagen is converted into gelatine and the meat becomes almost sticky in its succulence.

As we like our meat to be tender and juicy rather than dry and tough, it is important to cook it in such a way as to minimize fluid loss and to maximize the conversion of the tough collagen in the connective tissue into water-soluble gelatine.

It is possible to tenderize meat before cooking it. This can be done by damaging the meat physically: cutting, pounding and grinding to break down the structure of muscle bundles. It can also be done by marinating. The acid in citrus fruit or wine produces protein-digesting enzymes that can break down muscle and connective tissue.

POT-ROASTING

Pot-roasting is not really roasting at all but baking food enclosed in a pot, either in the oven or over a low heat. It is an old, economical method of cooking that was much used in the days before there were many domestic ovens. Roasting proper is a much faster, 'dry' method, used for cooking choicer, more tender cuts of meat and poultry by exposing them to direct heat. Pot-roasting involves cooking meat in its own juices and might better be called a simpler, quicker version of braising. It is ideal for cooking joints with plenty of connective tissue. A tender joint will toughen when pot-roasted or braised.

Traditionally there is very little liquid in a pot-roast, other than the fat needed for browning, as moisture from the meat provides most of the liquid during cooking.

A casserole with a tightly fitting lid creates a small oven. Steam is formed inside the pot from the moisture given off by the added liquid or by the food itself, and this tenderizes and cooks the meat. If the lid does not fit tightly, the steam can escape. Similarly, if the casserole or pan is too large, the liquid spreads over too large an area and is more likely to boil away. To make sure a lid fits tightly, cover the top of the pan with a piece of greaseproof paper and place the lid on top, jamming it down firmly.

If you have a flameproof casserole, you can brown meat on the hob and pot-roast in the oven in one vessel. Otherwise, brown the meat in a frying pan and transfer it with all the pan juices to a casserole for pot-roasting.

Coarsely cut root vegetables, raw or browned in the same fat as the meat, are sometimes placed under the meat. (The meat should be removed from the pan while browning the vegetables.) Once cooked, they can be served with the meat.

One way to ensure tender meat is to marinate it before cooking. A mixture of oil, wine and other flavourings penetrates the outer layer of the meat when it is left to marinate overnight in the refrigerator. The acid in the marinade also helps to break down tough fibres, and the oil prevents moisture evaporation and adds richness. Save some of the marinade to use as the cooking liquid.

Transfer the pot-roasted joint to a warmed serving dish or board to carve, and remove any strings or skewers. If there is too much liquid left in the pan, simply reduce it by boiling. Serve it separately.

GRILLING

Intense heat is the secret of successful grilling. Although this method requires active attention from the cook, its advantages are that the food cooks quickly and the charred surface gives great flavour.

To produce succulent, perfectly grilled meat with a crisp brown outside and pink juicy inside, it is absolutely essential to preheat the grill to its highest setting. This may take 10 or even 20 minutes for a grill on a good domestic cooker. Under a cooler grill, the meat's surface will not brown quickly, leaving the meat tasteless and unattractive by the time it is cooked through. If the grill cannot be adequately preheated to brown meat and fish quickly, save it for toast and fry the steaks instead.

It may take 2 hours before the embers of an open charcoal fire are flameless yet burn with the necessary intensity for grilling. Then, however, their fierce heat will cook a small lamb cutlet perfectly in 2 minutes and the charcoal will give it a wonderfully smoky flavour. Charcoal, when ready, glows bright red in the dark and has an ashy grey look in daylight.

Unlike braising, grilling will not tenderize meat, so only tender, choice cuts should be grilled. They should not be much thicker than 5cm/2 inches because of the high temperatures involved. Any thicker and the meat will remain cold and raw when the outside is black. Even so, unless the cut of meat is fairly thin, once it browns it must be moved further away from the heat source so that the interior can cook before the surface burns. Basting with the delicious pan juices or with olive oil adds flavour and shine. Turning is necessary for even cooking, and should be done halfway through the estimated cooking time, when the first surface is attractively brown.

When grilling over, rather than under, heat, use a fine grill rack or wire mesh grill to support delicate cuts of fish, and grease the grill rack or mesh well. Fish cuts can be wrapped in lightly greased foil and cooked over heat, but they then cook in their own steam rather than grill in the true sense.

The following points should be remembered when grilling:

1. Take food out of the refrigerator or freezer in plenty of time to have it at room temperature before grilling. An almost frozen steak will still be cold inside when the outside is brown and sizzling. This is particularly important if the steak is to be served very rare (blue).

2. Do not salt food much in advance. The salt draws moisture from the food. Salt after, during or immediately before grilling.

3. Brush the food with a minimum amount of oil to keep it moist and to speed the browning process. This is also essential to keep delicate foods such as fish from sticking.

4. The more well done meat or fish is, the tougher it will be to the touch and the palate.

5. To avoid piercing the meat and allowing the juices to escape, turn the grilling food with tongs or spoons, not a sharp instrument.

6. Serve immediately. Grilled food, even if well sealed, inevitably loses moisture, dries up and toughens if kept hot for any length of time.

GRILLING STEAKS
All grilled meats should be well browned on the surface, but the varying

degrees of 'doneness' are defined as follows:

BLUE   The inside is almost raw (but hot).

RARE   Red inside with plenty of red juices running freely.

MEDIUM RARE   As rare, but with fewer free-flowing juices and a paler centre.

MEDIUM   Pink in the centre with juices set.

WELL DONE   The centre is beige but the flesh is still juicy.

The best way to tell if meat is done is by its texture. Feel the meat by pressing firmly with a finger. Rare steak feels soft, almost raw; medium steak is firmer with some resilience to it; well done steak feels very firm. With practice there will soon be no need to cut and peep.

COOKING TIME FOR STEAKS varies with the heat of the grill, the distance of the food from the heat, the thickness of the cut and its fat content. The density of the meat also affects the cooking time. Open-textured steak, such as sirloin, will cook faster than the same thickness and weight of the closer textured rump.

GRILLING FISH

Lay the fish steaks and fillets on lightly greased foil on the grill rack, and set close under the preheated grill. This prevents the delicate flesh from sticking to the rack and breaking up when turned.

FRYING AND SAUTÉING

Frying, sometimes referred to as 'shallow frying', and sautéing are both quick cooking methods which are suitable for small, not-too-thick, tender pieces of meat and other foods. The difference between the two methods is the amount of fat used in cooking. For sautéing, an almost dry pan with no more than 15ml/1 tablespoon of fat is used; for frying, food is cooked in a little more fat unless using a non-stick frying pan, when virtually no fat at all is used.

The processes are similar to grilling, but when grilling small pieces of meat some fat is lost into the pan juices, which may or may not be eaten with the meat. In frying, the meat cooks in fat, at least some of which is eaten with the meat. For this reason the fat used for frying is an important consideration as its distinctive flavour – or the lack of it – will affect the taste of the dish. Olive oil will flavour fried foods, while corn, safflower, peanut and most other vegetable oils have little or no flavour.

FRYING

Techniques vary depending on the texture and size of the food and the effect the cook wishes to achieve. For instance, when frying steaks or chops remember to:

1. Fry in an uncovered wide pan. A lid traps the steam and the food stews or steams rather than frying crisply.

2. Preheat the fat. If the fat is cool when the food is put into it, the food will not brown. It will then lack flavour, look unattractive and might even absorb some of the cool fat and become too greasy.

3. Fry a little at a time. Adding too much food at one time to hot fat lowers the temperature and hinders the browning.

4. Fry fast until the meat is completely browned on all sides. Then turn down to a moderate heat to cook the inside through.

Fried food should be served as soon as possible after cooking. Juices gradually seep out and meat toughens on standing.

SAUTÉING is used on its own to cook foods such as chicken pieces, mushrooms or apple rings, but is most frequently used in conjunction with other forms of cooking. For example, whole small onions may be sautéd to brown them before they are added to liquid in a stew or a sauce.

Browning gives a sautéd dish its essential character. After browning, some meats, such as liver or veal slices, are often removed and then served with a relatively small amount of well flavoured sauce which has been made in the same pan. Meats such as pork chops or chicken pieces may be given an initial browning and then be cooked with added ingredients that will eventually form the sauce. The range of such sauces is almost endless – as various as the liquids and other flavourings that can be used in making them. Stages in sautéing are as follows:

1. Fry the main ingredient together with any others, browning them in minimal fat. Remove them from the pan and keep them hot.

2. Deglaze (see page 38) the pan with stock or wine.

3. Add the flavourings for the sauce.

4. If the initial browning has cooked the main ingredients sufficiently, reduce the sauce by rapid boiling and pour it over the dish. Garnish and serve immediately.

5. If the main ingredients need further cooking, simmer them in the sauce until they are tender, then proceed as above.

BRAISING

Braising, in the true sense of the word, is a method of slowly cooking meat on a mirepoix, a thick bed of finely diced mixed vegetables, with the addition of strong stock. In practice, the term braising is often confused with pot-roasting, as in both methods food is cooked slowly in a pan with a tightly fitting lid to give deliciously tender results. The main difference is that pot-roasted food is cooked with little, if any, liquid other than the fat used for browning the ingredients, while braising involves some liquid and at least some cut-up vegetables to add moisture to the pan, even if a true mirepoix is not used. A pot-roast should taste 'roasted', while a braise is closer to a stew.

Braising can also mean 'sweating'. This is a method of gently cooking vegetables, frequently onions and shallots, in oil in a covered pan, which is shaken frequently to prevent burning and sticking. Once cooked through, softened and exuding their juices but not coloured, the vegetables are usually added to stews, sauces or soups, to which they give a subtle flavouring but no colouring. For example, to 'braise' red cabbage, a finely chopped onion is sweated in oil until tender, then shredded cabbage, a little vinegar, sugar, apple and seasonings are added. These are left over a low heat, covered tightly, to sweat for 2–3 hours. The red cabbage is then 'braised', even though neither meat nor mirepoix have been included.

Occasionally, the term braising is used to mean baking in a covered pan with only a little liquid. Braised celery heart, for example, consists of quarters of celery head cooked in a little stock in a covered pan in the oven.

Beef fillet and sirloin or lamb best end should be roasted or grilled, but otherwise whole joints or smaller pieces of meat can with advantage be braised. The meat should be fairly lean and any fat that melts into the stock should be skimmed off before serving. Poultry may be braised unless it is old and tough, when stewing or poaching are more suitable cooking methods, as all the flesh, which will tend to be stringy and dry, is submerged in liquid.

The vegetables for the mirepoix should be browned quickly in a little hot fat and stirred constantly to ensure even colouring; then transferred to a heavy-based casserole or pan. The meat can be browned in the same fat before it is placed on top of the vegetables and stock is added. As the vegetables cook, they will disintegrate, helping to thicken the stock.

Making a strong, reduced, well-flavoured stock is time-consuming, but it is one of the key factors in good braising. The best stock is one made from chopped-up beef shin bones which have been browned all over and then simmered and skimmed frequently for hours (see page 151).

As with pot-roasting, meat may be marinated overnight in the refrigerator. Dry it well before browning.

The exacting and by no means easy steps for braising red meat to the ideal tenderness and almost sticky juiciness are as follows:

1. Fry the mirepoix of vegetables in oil, shaking the pan and stirring until they are evenly browned all over.

2. Brown the meat on all sides and place it on top of the vegetable bed in a heavy casserole.

3. Add stock, made from gelatinous meats such as knuckle of veal or beef shin bones, to cover the meat. If the stock is not rich and solidly set when cold, the braise will not have the correct 'melting' stickiness. Then stew, without basting, until half-cooked.

4. Lift out the meat, strain the stock, and discard the mirepoix, which will by now have imparted all its flavour.

5. Return the meat to the casserole and reduce the stock by rapid boiling until it is thick and syrupy, then pour it over the meat.

6. There will no longer be enough stock to cover the meat and there is a danger, even in a covered pan, of the exposed top drying out, so turn the meat every 15 minutes and baste it with the stock.

By the end of the cooking time, when the meat is tender, the stock should be so reduced as to provide a shiny coating that will not run off the meat. It will penetrate the flesh, moistening it and giving it the slightly glutinous texture of perfectly braised meat.

STEWING

The term 'stew' is so widely used that it can mean almost anything. A 'stew' is essentially food that has been slowly and gently cooked in plenty of liquid. Most cooks envisage meat cut into smallish pieces before cooking but the term is sometimes used for sliced, sautéed meat or poultry served in a sauce, or for a whole joint or bird poached in liquid. Many stews require preliminary frying of the meat, and sometimes of onions, shallots, carrots or mushrooms too. This gives a richer flavour to the ingredients and adds colour and flavour to the sauce, which will be made on top of the browned sediment and dried-on juices sticking to the pan after frying. These are called 'brown' stews. 'White' stews are made without preliminary browning and are less rich, less fatty, altogether gentler and more easily digestible than brown ones.

Both brown and white stews are served in their cooking liquid, which is usually thickened to a syrupy sauce.

The principles of shallow-frying (see page 48–49) apply to the preliminary frying for a brown stew. If the sauce is not to taste insipid, or be pale in colour, you must start with a good, even colour on both sides of each slice or all sides of each cube of meat. Good stews are

made or lost in the early stages – so take care to fry only a few pieces at a time, to keep the temperature hot enough to sizzle and to take the time to get an even colour. Deglaze the pan as often as necessary. Deglazing serves three essential purposes: it prevents the stuck sediment in the pan from burning; it allows the flavour of that sediment to be captured and incorporated into the sauce; and it cleans the pan ready for the next batch of meat.

BOILING AND POACHING

BOILING is a blanket term for cooking food submerged in liquid by one of several techniques: from fast, agitated bubbling – a rolling boil – to a gentle simmer, when bubbles will appear in one part of the pan only, or to the barest tremble of the liquid, which is poaching. The techniques suit different foods and achieve different effects.

Cooking green vegetables quickly in rapidly boiling water in an open pan tenderizes them, yet makes sure they retain their crispness and bright colour. The water should be well salted (15ml/1 level tablespoon for every 1.75 litres/3 pints), as it then boils at a higher temperature, cooking the vegetables even more quickly.

Rapid boiling in an open pan protects the vivid colours of some vegetables, such as artichokes, while enhancing the colours of others, such as peas and spinach. When covered, discoloration can be caused by enzymes from the vegetables, which collect in the condensation on the lid and fall back into the water. The best method is to bring the water to the boil without the vegetables, add the vegetables and cover with a lid to bring them back to the boil as fast as possible, then remove the lid to allow the escape of steam.

Vegetables that would be damaged by vigorous boiling are cooked by the more gentle simmering methods. Vegetables unlikely to discolour, such as potatoes, carrots, parsnips, beetroot and other root vegetables, are traditionally cooked in a covered pan to preserve heat and contain fuel costs. Hence the adage: 'If it grows in the light, cook it in the open; if it grows in the dark, keep it covered.'

REFRESHING Once cooked, 'refresh' the vegetables by rinsing them briefly under cold water, then put them in a warm serving dish. 'Refreshing' prevents further cooking by the heat retained in the vegetables, and thus sets the colour. Vegetables that hold their colour well, such as carrots, or small quantities of vegetables, such as French beans for four people, do not need refreshing, but for large quantities it is vital, especially if there is to be any delay before serving. They can be reheated briefly before serving by any of the following methods: by being dipped in boiling water; by rapid steaming; by being given 30–60 seconds in a microwave oven; by being tossed quickly in oil over high heat. Slow reheating in the oven will discolour most green vegetables, frozen peas being the exception, although even these will eventually lose their brilliant hue.

BLANCHING Some foods, especially vegetables and fruit, are immersed in boiling water without being fully cooked. This is called 'blanching' and has various uses:

1. To remove strong flavours, e.g. from liver or kidneys before frying.
2. To facilitate the removal of skin, e.g. from tomatoes or peaches.
3. To lessen the salt content, e.g. from ham before cooking.
4. To destroy enzymes in vegetables destined for the freezer and to prevent discoloration.
5. To shorten the roasting time of vegetables, such as potatoes, onions and parsnips, by parboiling first.
6. Simply to semi-cook or soften food, e.g. fennel for salad.

FAST BOILING Rice and pasta cook well at a good rolling boil. The boiling water expands the starch granules and makes them tender, while the rapid agitation keeps the pieces of pasta or rice grains from sticking together or to the pan. Adding 15ml/1 tablespoon of oil to the water also helps to prevent sticking. Long-grain rice boiled in a large pan of heavily salted water takes 10–11 minutes to cook. The grains should then mash to a paste when pressed between the thumb and index finger, though a little 'bite' is preferable to an all-over soft texture.

Similarly, pasta should always be cooked *al dente*, i.e. firm to the bite. Remember that fresh or home-made pasta, which already contains moisture, cooks four times faster than the dried commercial equivalents. The cooking time also depends on the thickness. Dried vermicelli cooks in 2–3 minutes, while dried lasagne takes 15–16 (see page 171–173).

Sometimes rapid boiling is used to drive off moisture and reduce liquids to a thicker consistency. With sugar mixtures, the essential high temperatures are most rapidly achieved by a galloping boil.

SIMMERING Dried pulses are also cooked by boiling. As there is no colour loss to worry about, and the process is a long one, they may be simmered rather than fast-boiled. Rapidly boiling water evaporates very fast, risking boiling dry and burning. Pulses may even, with advantage, be slowly stewed – cooked in a covered pan in liquid that only partially covers them – either on top of the stove or in the oven. If the proportion of liquid to pulses is right, they absorb all the liquid during cooking. There is nothing to throw away and little loss of taste and nutrients. The amount of water needed obviously depends on the age, and therefore dryness, of the pulses and the speed of boiling, but twice the volume of water to pulses is a good guide.

It is often recommended that pulses be soaked in water before cooking, but this is not always necessary, especially if the pulses are last season's crop. Dried beans that are known to be 2–3 years old can be cooked without any prior soaking, but they will absorb more water, take longer to become tender, and will not taste as good as fresher pulses. As a general rule, soaking is a good idea, especially for the larger beans.

Pressure-cooking works well for pulses and eliminates the need for soaking. Pressure cookers vary and it is obviously sensible to consult the manufacturer's instructions. As a general rule, 450g/1lb of dried peas or beans, unsoaked, will need 1 litre/1¾ pints water and will cook in 30 minutes at 8kg/15lb pressure.

POACHING is also long, slow, gentle cooking, but the food is generally completely submerged in liquid that is barely trembling, either on top of the stove or in the oven. It is an excellent method for delicate items, such as fish or soft fruit, which would break up if subjected to vigorous agitation.

Tough meat becomes more tender and succulent the more slowly it is cooked. A cut such as oxtail takes at least 3 hours of simmering on top of the stove until it is acceptably tender. Poached in the oven at 150°C/300°F/gas mark 2 for 5 hours, it would be even more tender, falling from the bone and gelatinous.

STEAMING

Steaming is the cooking of food in hot vapours over boiling liquid (usually water) rather than in liquid. It occurs to some extent in braising and pot-roasting because of the closed pans and the relatively small amounts of liquid used. In true steaming, however, the food never touches the liquid, so the loss of many vitamins is significantly reduced. Furthermore, steamed food is not browned first, so it can be cooked without fat. This makes the food more easily digestible and particularly suitable for invalids and those on low-fat diets. Excellent ingredients are essential for steaming – there is no help to be had from browning, so the food must taste good without such assistance.

A variety of equipment for steaming food is available. Most common are oval or round steamers, which are like double saucepans, except that the top has holes in its base. Steam from boiling water in the lower pan rises through the holes to cook the food, while the lid on the upper pan keeps in the steam.

Another popular steaming device is a stainless steel or aluminium basket that opens and folds shut and is used with an ordinary lidded saucepan. The basket stands on its own short legs to keep it clear of the boiling water. It fits inside most saucepans and is particularly suitable for foods that do not need much cooking time as the water underneath the short legs would otherwise have to be replaced too frequently. The saucepan must have a tightly fitting lid.

VEGETABLES are the food most commonly steamed as they cook quickly and retain more of their colour and texture this way. Careful timing is essential as steamed food can be tasteless if even slightly overcooked. Steaming times for vegetables are short, giving bright-coloured, *al dente*, palpably fresh results. Some vegetables can be steamed in their own juices.

Spinach, for example, may be trimmed and put wet from washing into a covered saucepan over medium heat, and shaken occasionally until limp and cooked, but still very green. This takes 3–5 minutes.

Potatoes that tend to break up when boiled before they are cooked are best steamed; choose potatoes that are about the same size, as they cook at the same time. If they are very large or of different sizes, cut them into bite-sized pieces before steaming. For most other root vegetables, such as turnips, parsnips and swedes, cut them into 1cm/ ½ inch dice and steam them until tender before seasoning and serving.

FISH AND POULTRY Steaming fish is simple and quick and always produces a delicate result if the fish is not allowed to overcook. Put the food on a piece of muslin or cheesecloth to prevent it sticking to the steamer bottom. Oval steamers and folding baskets are suitable for small quantities of fish, but for larger fish or cooking many small fish, shellfish, fish steaks or fillets, a fish kettle (usually used for poaching fish) may be used. Made of metal, these come in sizes to take whole fish on a perforated rack inside the kettle. Ramekins can be placed under the rack to keep it well above the boiling liquid. Whole fish can be stuffed and cooked over liquid in a covered kettle on top of the stove. Allow about 8 minutes per 450g/1lb of fish.

Delicate poultry such as chicken breasts or whole small quail may be steamed similarly.

Plate steaming is an excellent method of cooking small quantities of fish in their own juices. Put the fish fillets or steaks on a plate, season well and cover with another upturned plate or tin foil. Set the covered plate on top of a pan of gently boiling water or on a trivet inside a large frying pan of bubbling water and cook for 8–10 minutes, depending on the thickness of the fish.

Fat content of various foods

Bacon	Fat (g/100g)
Collar joint, boiled, lean and fat	27.0
Collar joint, boiled, lean only	9.7
Gammon, boiled or grilled, lean and fat	18.9
Gammon, boiled or grilled, lean only	5.5
Rashers, grilled, lean only	18.9
Rashers, back, lean and fat	33.8
Rashers, streaky, lean and fat	36.0
Rashers, middle, lean and fat	35.1

Beef	
Brisket, boiled, lean and fat	23.9
Forerib, roast, lean and fat	28.8
Forerib, roast, lean only	12.6
Rump steak, grilled, lean and fat	12.1
Rump steak, grilled, lean only	6.0
Stewing steak, lean and fat	11.0
Topside, roast, lean and fat	12.0
Topside, roast, lean only	4.4

Lamb	
Breast, roast, lean and fat	37.1
Breast, roast, lean only	16.6
Chops, grilled, lean and fat without bone	29.0
Chops, grilled, lean only without bone	12.3
Leg, roast, lean and fat	17.9
Leg, roast, lean only	8.1
Scrag and neck, stewed, lean and fat	21.1
Scrag and neck, stewed, lean only	15.7

Pork	Fat (g/100g)
Chops, grilled, lean and fat without bone	24.2
Chops, grilled, lean only without bone	10.7
Leg, roast, lean and fat	19.8
Leg, roast, lean only	6.9

Veal	
Cutlets, grilled	5.0
Fillet, roast	11.5

Chicken	
Roast, meat and skin	14.0
Roast, meat only	5.5

Grouse	
Roast	3–5

Partridge	
Roast	4–7

Pheasant	
Roast	5–10

Pigeon	
Roast	5–13

Turkey	
Roast, meat and skin	6.5
Roast, meat only	2.7

Rabbit	
Stewed	3–7

Hare	
Stewed	3–7

Offal	Fat (g/100g)
Hearts, stewed	3–6
Kidneys	5–7
Liver, grilled, etc.	5

Cooking fat	Total fat content (g/100g)
Butter	82.0
Margarine	82.0
Gold	40.7
Outline	40.7
Low-fat spreads	40.7
Cream, single	21.2
Cream, soured	21.2
Cream, whipping	35.0
Cream, double	48.2

Cheese	
Camembert, Brie, etc.	23.2
Cheddar, Cheshire, Gruyère, Emmental, etc.	33.5
Danish Blue, Roquefort, etc.	29.2
Edam, Gouda, St Paulin, etc.	22.9
Parmesan	29.7
Stilton	40.0
Cream cheese	47.4
Low-fat Cottage Cheese (see carton)	0–4
Medium-fat Curd Cheese	25.0
Medium-fat Mozzarella, etc.	25.0

Fish	Fat (g/100g)
Eel, stewed	13.2
Herring, grilled	13.0
Bloater, grilled	12.9
Kipper, baked	6.2
Mackerel, grilled	6.2
Salmon, steamed	13.0
Sardines, canned (drained)	13.0
Sprats, grilled (estimated value)	13.0
Trout, steamed	3.0
Tuna, canned (includes oil)	22.0
Tuna, canned (drained, estimated value)	13.0

Tomato and Red Pepper Soup

Chicken and Spring Vegetable Broth

Mediterranean Toasts with Spicy Prawn and Squid Tapas

Asparagus and Dill in Jelly

Lime-marinated Salmon with Papaya

White Fish Rostis with Salsa Verde

Trout with Coriander and Mint Relish

Roast Cod with Garlic

SOUPS

SOUPS

POTATO AND GARLIC SOUP

SERVES 4

PER PORTION Energy: 803kj/191kcal
Fat: 9.0g Saturated fat: 1.2g

3 tablespoons olive oil
8 garlic cloves, unpeeled
1 onion, chopped
450g/1lb potatoes, peeled and sliced
generous pinch saffron
salt and freshly ground black pepper
1.6 litres/2½ pints chicken or vegetable
  stock (see pages 152 and 154)
1 tablespoon chopped parsley

1. In a small saucepan heat the olive oil with the garlic and cook gently for 20 minutes. Do not brown the garlic. Remove from the heat and leave to infuse for a further 20 minutes.
2. Strain the olive oil through a fine sieve and reserve. Peel the garlic cloves.
3. Heat the infused olive oil in a heavy-bottomed pan and cook the onion until soft but not coloured.
4. Add the potatoes, garlic, saffron, salt and pepper and the stock. Simmer until the potatoes are soft.
5. Liquidize the soup and push it through a sieve.

6. Pour into the rinsed-out saucepan. Season to taste and add water if the soup is too thick. Stir in the chopped parsley and reheat carefully.

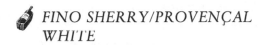 *FINO SHERRY/PROVENÇAL WHITE*

CARAMELIZED PARSNIP, APPLE AND PECAN NUT SOUP

SERVES 4

PER PORTION Energy: 966kj/230kcal
Fat: 8.8g Saturated fat: 1.1g

1 tablespoon olive or walnut oil
1 Spanish onion, chopped
675g/1½lb medium parsnips, peeled
  and chopped
1 Bramley apple, peeled and chopped
1 tablespoon soft brown sugar
½ tablespoon balsamic vinegar
1 tablespoon Madeira
570ml/1 pint good chicken stock (see
  page 152)
salt and freshly ground black pepper
nutmeg

To serve:
15g/½oz Parmesan, grated
15g/½oz pecan nuts, toasted and
  chopped

1. Heat the oil in a large, heavy-bottomed saucepan, add the onion and cook until nearly soft but not coloured.
2. Add the parsnips, stir and cook, covered, for 20 minutes.
3. When beginning to soften, add the apple and cook, stirring occasionally, until softened.
4. Remove the lid and add the sugar. Increase the heat and cook, stirring all the time, until the parsnips and apple

are a rich caramel colour but not burnt.
5. Stir in the balsamic vinegar and Madeira, then add the chicken stock. Season with salt, pepper and nutmeg, bring to the boil and simmer for 10 minutes.
6. Liquidize the soup.
7. Reheat in the rinsed-out saucepan. Season to taste and add water if the soup is too thick.
8. Serve sprinkled with the grated Parmesan and chopped pecan nuts.

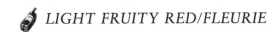 *LIGHT FRUITY RED/FLEURIE*

TOMATO AND RED PEPPER SOUP

SERVES 4

PER PORTION Energy: 448kj/107kcal
Fat 6.6g Saturated fat 1.0g

1 tablespoon sunflower oil
1 onion, finely chopped
1 red pepper, deseeded and finely
   chopped
570ml/1 pint passata
dash Tabasco sauce
2 drops Worcestershire sauce
30g/1oz white rice
290ml/½ pint water
salt and freshly ground black pepper

To serve:
2 teaspoons low-fat natural yoghurt
2 teaspoons red pesto sauce (see page
   161)

1. Heat the oil in a saucepan and sweat
the onion and pepper until soft.
2. Add the passata, Tabasco,
Worcestershire sauce, rice, water, salt
and pepper and cook for 25 minutes, or
until the rice is soft.
3. Place the soup in a food processor or
liquidizer and blend until smooth.
Return to the pan and leave to simmer
for 5 minutes. Taste and season, if
necessary.
4. Mix together the yoghurt and pesto
sauce and add to the soup, off the heat,
just before serving.

 *AUSTRALIAN CHARDONNAY*

61

BEETROOT AND GINGER SOUP

SERVES 4

PER PORTION Energy: 454kj/108kcal
Fat: 3.4g Saturated fat: 0.4g

1 tablespoon sunflower oil
1 onion, chopped
1 carrot, peeled and chopped
½ teaspoon ground cumin
½ teaspoon ground ginger
1 garlic clove, crushed
1 × 5cm/2in piece fresh ginger, peeled
  and grated
450g/1lb cooked fresh beetroot, peeled
  and roughly chopped
860ml/1½ pints chicken stock (see page
  152)
salt and freshly ground black pepper
1 tablespoon cider vinegar
1 tablespoon vodka (optional)

To serve:
4 tablespoons light Greek yoghurt
chopped chives, dill or coriander

1. In a heavy-bottomed saucepan heat
the oil and cook the onion and carrot
until soft but not coloured. Stir in the
ground cumin, ground ginger, crushed
garlic and half the fresh ginger. Cook,
stirring, for 1 minute.
2. Add the beetroot and stock, season
with salt and pepper, bring back to the
boil, reduce and simmer for 20 minutes.
3. Process or liquidize the mixture and
sieve into the rinsed-out saucepan.

4. When ready to serve, reheat without
boiling, then taste and season if
necessary. Add the remaining fresh
ginger to taste.
5. Pour into individual soup bowls, add
a spoonful of yoghurt and sprinkle with
the herbs.

 *LIGHT ALSACE WHITE/TOKAY*

YELLOW PEPPER AND BARLEY SOUP

SERVES 4

PER PORTION Energy: 843kj/201kcal
Fat: 4.0g Saturated fat: 0.5g

1 tablespoon olive oil
2 Spanish onions, finely chopped
4 yellow peppers
2 garlic cloves, crushed
sprig of thyme
110g/4oz barley, soaked in water
  overnight
1.2 litres/2 pints strong chicken stock
  (see page 152)
salt and freshly ground black pepper
1 tablespoon cider vinegar

For the garnish:
chopped parsley

1. Set the oven to 200°C/400°F/gas
mark 6.
2. Heat the oil in a saucepan, add the
onions and cook until soft but not
coloured.
3. Put the peppers on a baking sheet and
roast in the oven for about 15 minutes,
turning once, until they are soft and the
skins shrivelled and black. Allow to
cool completely in a sealed plastic or
paper bag.
4. Add the garlic, thyme and barley to
the onions, stir and cook for 2 minutes.
5. Pour in the stock and bring slowly to
the boil. Reduce the heat and simmer
for about 15 minutes.

6. When the peppers are cool, peel off
the skins and remove the stalks,
membrane and seeds. Pour any juices
into the saucepan. Chop the peppers
and add to the soup. Cook for a further
20–30 minutes.
7. When the barley is tender, taste and
season with salt and pepper.
8. Just before serving add the cider
vinegar and garnish with chopped
parsley.

 *WHITE LOIRE/SAUVIGNON*

LENTIL, TOMATO AND LEMON SOUP

SERVES 4

PER PORTION Energy 1094kj/260kcal
Fat: 4.3g Saturated fat: 0.5g

1 tablespoon sunflower oil
1 Spanish onion, chopped
2 medium carrots, chopped
1 celery stalk, chopped
225g/8oz orange lentils
1 garlic clove, crushed
860ml/1½ pints strong chicken stock
  (see page 152)
1 bay leaf
5ml/1 teaspoon tomato purée
salt and freshly ground black pepper
450g/1lb large tomatoes, peeled,
  deseeded and chopped
grated zest of ½ lemon
juice of 1 lemon
1 tablespoon chopped coriander

1. Heat the oil in a saucepan, add the onions and cook until soft but not coloured.
2. Add the carrots and celery and cook until soft.
3. Wash the lentils, drain well and put into the pan with the garlic, chicken stock, bay leaf, tomato purée and pepper. Bring to the boil, reduce the heat and simmer for 20–30 minutes, or until the lentils are really tender.
4. When the lentils are soft, remove the bay leaf and process or liquidize the mixture until smooth.

5. Return the soup to the rinsed-out saucepan, add the tomatoes, lemon zest and juice, and reheat. Add the coriander. Season to taste with salt and pepper and pour into individual soup bowls.

 *BEAUJOLAIS/LIGHT FRUITY RED*

CHICKEN AND SPRING VEGETABLE BROTH

SERVES 4

PER PORTION Energy: 877kj/209kcal
Fat: 4.2g Saturated fat: 1.2g

225g/8oz cooked chicken
1 courgette, halved and sliced on the
*   diagonal*
110g/4oz frozen peas
1.2 litres/2 pints good chicken stock (see
*   page 152)*
110g/4oz small pasta (for soups)
150ml/½ pint water
salt and freshly ground black pepper
cider vinegar, to taste

To serve:
2 teaspoons basil pesto (see page 160)
shavings of Parmesan, or fresh sprigs of
*   basil*

1. Skin the chicken and pull the flesh
into bite-sized pieces.
2. In a pan of boiling salted water,
cook the courgette and peas for 4
minutes. Drain and refresh under cold
water.
3. Bring the chicken stock to the boil in
a large saucepan. Add the pasta and
cook until nearly *al dente*.
4. Reduce the heat, then add the water,
chicken pieces, courgettes and peas.
Heat through, but do not boil.
5. Taste, season with salt and pepper,
and vinegar if desired.
6. Serve in individual bowls, swirling

the pesto on top and sprinkling with
Parmesan or fresh sprigs of basil.

 *SAUVIGNON/SOAVE*

MISCELLANEOUS FIRST COURSES

MISCELLANEOUS FIRST COURSES

GRILLED AUBERGINES WITH CHICK PEA PASTE

SERVES 4

PER PORTION Energy: 662kj/158kcal
Fat: 6.4g Saturated fat: 0.5g

1 large aubergine, cut into 8 round slices
1 × 400g/14oz tin chick peas, drained
and rinsed
½ teaspoon ground cumin
1 garlic clove, crushed
juice of ½ lemon
1 tablespoon chopped flat-leaf parsley
2 tablespoons hot water (optional)
salt and freshly ground black pepper
110g/4oz fresh cherry tomatoes, halved

For the marinade:
1 tablespoon honey
2 tablespoons balsamic vinegar
2 dessertspoons sesame oil
juice ½ lemon
pinch of cayenne
¼ tablespoon ground cumin
¼ tablespoon ground coriander

1. Sprinkle the aubergine with salt and leave to drain in a colander for 30 minutes. Rinse thoroughly and dry on absorbent paper. Place in a bowl or plastic bag.
2. Mix the marinade ingredients together, pour over the aubergines and stir carefully to coat. Leave to marinade for at least 2 hours or overnight. Baste or stir frequently.
3. Place the chick peas, cumin, garlic, lemon juice and half the parsley in a food processor. Purée until smooth. Add a little of the marinade or 2 tablespoons hot water to produce a soft cream. Season to taste.
4. Heat the grill to its highest setting.
5. Lift the aubergines from the marinade and drain well.
6. Grill the aubergines for about 6 minutes on each side, or until soft and pale brown.
7. Spoon the chick pea purée on to one side of the aubergines and return to the grill for 4 more minutes.
8. Arrange on plates, garnished with the tomatoes and remaining parsley.

 *LIGHT RED*

MEDITERRANEAN TOASTS

SERVES 4

PER PORTION Energy: 929kj/222kcal
Fat 7.5g Saturated fat 1.0g

For the aubergine pâté:
1 small aubergine
1 garlic clove, peeled
1 bay leaf
3 sprigs thyme
1 tablespoon Greek yoghurt
1 large handful parsley, chopped finely
2 teaspoons olive oil
2 teaspoons lemon juice
salt and freshly ground black pepper

For the garlic cheese spread:
1 large handful parsley, chopped
½ garlic clove, crushed
85g/3oz skimmed milk soft cheese
salt and freshly ground black pepper

For the pepper salad:
1 red pepper
1 yellow pepper
2 teaspoons olive oil
salt and freshly ground black pepper

To serve:
12 thin slices French bread
green salad

1. Make the aubergine pâté: preheat the oven to 200°C/400°F/gas mark 6.
2. Remove the stalk from the aubergine. Cut lengthways slits 1cm/½ inch apart leaving about 2cm/¾ inch uncut at either end. Cut the garlic clove into thin slivers and insert with the bay leaf and thyme into the slits.
3. Wrap the aubergine tightly in tin foil and bake in the oven for about 30 minutes or until soft. Allow to cool slightly.
4. Remove the garlic, bay leaf and thyme then process the aubergine, yoghurt, parsley, oil, lemon juice, salt and black pepper in a food processor or liquidizer. Place in a bowl and when cool, place in the refrigerator and leave to chill.
5. Make the garlic cheese spread: Mix together the parsley, garlic, cheese, salt and pepper in a bowl. Refrigerate.
6. Make the pepper salad: Heat the oven to 200°C/400°F/gas mark 6. Place the peppers on a baking sheet and bake in the oven for about 15 minutes, turning once, until they are soft and the skins are shrivelled and black. Place the peppers in a plastic bag, close and leave for 20 minutes. Allow to cool. Pour any juices that have accumulated in the bag into a mixing bowl. Peel off the skins, then discard the stalks, membrane and seeds.
7. Cut the flesh into thin strips and mix with the reserved juices, oil, salt and pepper in a bowl. Chill until ready to serve.
8. To serve: toast the French bread on both sides under the grill. Spread 4 slices with the aubergine pâté, 4 slices with the garlic cheese spread and divide the pepper salad between the remaining 4 slices. Give each person 1 slice of each of the different toppings and serve the green salad separately.

 *VIN DE PAYS/ROSÉ*

TOMATO SORBET

SERVES 4

PER PORTION (with avocado pear ice)
Energy: 890kj/219kcal Fat: 15.9g
Saturated fat: trace.

½ tablespoon shredded basil
½ tablespoon chopped fresh parsley
550g/1lb 4oz passata
1 tablespoon Worcestershire sauce
Tabasco, to taste
pinch of sugar
squeeze of lemon juice
1 tablespoon vodka (optional)
salt and freshly ground black pepper
2 egg whites

To serve:
avocado pear ice (see page 72)
basil leaves

1. Mix the basil and parsley with the passata and season with the Worcestershire sauce, Tabasco, sugar, lemon juice, vodka (if using), salt and pepper. Transfer to a container and freeze.
2. When nearly frozen, put the sorbet into a liquidizer or food processor and whiz briefly. Gradually add the unwhisked egg white to the mixture and whiz again: it will fluff up tremendously. Taste and season as necessary. Return to the container and freeze until firm.
3. To serve, remove from the freezer 30 minutes in advance; serve with the avocado pear ice and garnish with fresh basil.

 *SPICY DRY WHITE*

AVOCADO PEAR ICE

SERVES 4

PER PORTION (with tomato sorbet)
Energy: 890kj/219kcal Fat: 15.9g
Saturated fat: trace

2 avocado pears
1 tablespoon chopped fresh coriander
½ teaspoon ground coriander
juice of ½ lime
Tabasco (optional)
salt and freshly ground pepper

To serve:
tomato sorbet (see page 71)
basil leaves

1. Peel the avocado pears, remove the stones and mash the flesh with a fork.
2. Stir in the fresh and ground coriander, the lime juice and Tabasco (if using). Taste and season with salt and pepper. Transfer to a container and freeze.
3. When almost frozen, whisk until smooth and return to the freezer.
4. An hour before serving, remove from the freezer and allow to soften. Serve with tomato sorbet.

 *SPICY DRY WHITE*

BAKED BULBS OF GARLIC

SERVES 4

PER PORTION Energy: 233kj/55kcal
Fat: 3.0g Saturated fat: 0.4g

4 whole heads of garlic
1 tablespoon olive oil
½ tablespoon fresh chopped rosemary
salt and freshly ground black pepper

To serve:
crusty bread or ciabatta

1. Heat the oven to 180°C/350°F/gas mark 4.
2. Slice the bulbs of garlic in half horizontally, brush the cut sides with the olive oil and sprinkle with rosemary, salt and pepper.
3. Place cut side up in an ovenproof dish, then pour in 5mm/¼ inch water. Cover with a lid, or foil and bake in the oven for 30 minutes. Remove the cover and bake for a further 30 minutes, or until the garlic cloves are tender.
4. Lift the bulbs of garlic from the dish with a slotted spoon. Drizzle with extra olive oil (optional).
5. To serve: Allow a head of garlic per person; at the table the pulp is squeezed out of each garlic skin and spread on to warm crusty bread. Finger bowls or napkins may be required.

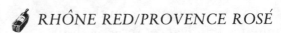 *RHÔNE RED/PROVENCE ROSÉ*

ASPARAGUS AND DILL IN JELLY

SERVES 4

PER PORTION Energy: 206kj/49kcal
Fat: 0.8g Saturated fat: none

675g/1½lb fresh fine asparagus
570ml/1 pint well-flavoured aspic (see
 page 155)
1 tablespoon chopped dill

1. Trim and wash the asparagus.
2. In a pan of boiling salted water, cook the asparagus until tender, about 6 minutes. (For this dish the asparagus should be quite tender.)
3. Drain the asparagus and refresh under cold water until cold. Dry on absorbent paper. Trim to the length of a 1.2 litre/2 pint loaf tin.
4. Melt the aspic very gently, then add the dill. Pour about 5mm/¼ inch into the base of a well-chilled loaf tin. Leave to set.
5. When set, arrange some asparagus spears head to tail in a tight single layer on the jelly. Stir the remaining aspic, pour in enough to come a quarter of the way up the asparagus and leave in the refrigerater to set. Arrange another layer of asparagus on the jelly and repeat the process, finishing with a smooth layer of aspic. The tin should be very tightly packed. Leave to become completely set.
6. To turn out the jelly, dip the outside of the tin briefly in hot water. Invert a wet plate over the jelly mould, then turn tin and plate over together. Give a sharp shake and remove the mould.

NOTE: The aspic must always be stirred before it is poured into the tin to ensure that the dill is evenly distributed.

 *MEDIUM WHITE*

LEEK AND ARTICHOKE MOUSSE

SERVES 4

PER PORTION Energy: 445kj/106kcal
Fat: 3.9g Saturated fat 0.4g

1 tablespoon sunflower oil
340g/12oz leeks, thinly sliced
1 teaspoon Dijon mustard
2 tablespoons artichoke paste
½ tablespoon powdered gelatine
2 tablespoons water
200g/7oz quark
salt and freshly ground black pepper

For the garnish:
watercress

1. Heat the oil in a saucepan and cook the leeks until very soft but not coloured. Drain in a sieve over a bowl to remove any excess oil.
2. Process the leeks until smooth, then add the mustard and artichoke paste and process again. Chill well.
3. In a small saucepan soak the gelatine in 2 tablespoons water.
4. Oil 4 ramekin dishes and leave to drain upside-down.
5. Stir the quark with a spoon until smooth, then add the cold purée. Season to taste with salt and pepper.
6. Heat the gelatine and, when melted, stir into the mixture.
7. Pile into the ramekin dishes. Cover and chill for at least 4 hours.
8. To serve: Turn out the mousses on to individual plates and garnish with watercress.

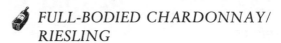 *FULL-BODIED CHARDONNAY/ RIESLING*

YAKITORI-STYLE SKEWERS

This recipe calls for Japanese soy sauce; if it is not available, light soy sauce is the best substitute. If you can't find mirin (rice wine), light muscovado sugar or a sweet sherry can be used in its place.

SERVES 4

PER PORTION Energy: 727kj/173kcal
Fat: 7.1g Saturated fat: 1.4g

2 chicken breasts
grated zest of ½ lemon
½ tablespoon chopped chives
pinch ground cumin
freshly ground black pepper
2 red onions, quartered

For the sauce:
2 tablespoons dry sherry
3 tablespoons Japanese soy sauce
1 tablespoon mirin (Japanese rice wine)
1 teaspoon sugar

To serve:
oakleaf lettuce or red chicory
2 tablespoons French dressing (see page 163)

1. Place 8 wooden skewers in water and soak them for 1 hour or overnight.
2. Trim the chicken and cut into finger-length strips. Mix with the lemon zest, chives, cumin and pepper, then cover and refrigerate for at least 30 minutes or overnight.
3. Divide each onion quarter into two. Thread the chicken strips and onion alternately on the 8 skewers.
4. Preheat the grill to a medium setting.
5. Mix all the sauce ingredients together.
6. When ready to serve, put the skewered chicken on a baking sheet, pour over a little of the sauce and grill for about 6 minutes on each side, pouring over more sauce as they grill. They are ready when the chicken is opaque and the onion soft.
7. To serve: Toss the salad leaves in the French dressing and place on a serving dish. Arrange the Yakitori-style skewers on top and pour over any remaining sauce.

 *SEMILLON*

CHICKEN CAKES WITH TOMATO AND GINGER SAUCE

These chicken cakes make a very good main course, if the quantities are doubled.

SERVES 4

PER PORTION (without sauce)
Energy: 731.5kj/174.2kcal Fat: 7.5g
Saturated fat: 1.2g (with sauce) Energy:
986kj/235kcal Fat: 10.5g
Saturated fat: 1.7g

225g/8oz lean chicken, skinned and
boned (see page 111–114)
2 large shallots, chopped
450g/1lb parsnips, peeled and parboiled
110g/4oz celeriac, peeled and blanched
1 tablespoon sunflower oil
1 tablespoon chopped coriander
½ tablespoon sesame seeds, toasted

For the marinade:
2 teaspoons medium sherry
1 teaspoon light soy sauce
1 teaspoon sesame oil
grated zest of 1 lemon
2.5cm/1 inch fresh ginger, grated
2 garlic cloves, crushed

To serve:
tomato and ginger sauce (see page 157)

1. Trim the chicken, place in a food processor and mince finely. Transfer to a bowl with the shallots. Mix all the marinade ingredients together, pour over the chicken and shallots, then cover and refrigerate for 1 hour or overnight.
2. Grate the parsnips and celeriac into a bowl. Set aside.
3. Drain off and discard any excess marinade. Heat the oil in a frying pan, add the chicken and shallots, and stir constantly until opaque. Remove from the heat and mix with the parsnips, celeriac, coriander and sesame seeds. Season with salt and pepper.
4. Heat the grill to a medium setting.
5. With wet hands, shape the chicken mixture into four cakes and place on a baking sheet. Grill for 3–4 minutes on both sides. Serve hot, handing the tomato and ginger sauce separately.

NOTE: If it is difficult to shape the chicken mixture into cakes, add ½ an egg white to bind it together.

 *LIGHT RED*

CHICKEN LIVER AND SHIITAKE MUSHROOM SALAD

SERVES 4 as a first course; for a main course increase the quantities by half.

PER PORTION Energy: 1324kj/314kcal
Fat: 20.6g Saturated fat: 3.7g

450g/1lb chicken livers
1 tablespoon olive oil
1 head of garlic, unpeeled but split into
   cloves
225g/8oz shiitake or field mushrooms,
   sliced
pinch each of garam masala, cayenne,
   ground cumin and coriander
30g/1oz dried ceps, soaked in 60ml/4
   tablespoons hot water for 30 minutes
sprig of thyme
1 tablespoon balsamic vinegar
85g/3oz seedless grapes
salt and freshly ground black pepper

To serve:
mixed salad leaves
3 tablespoons French dressing, made
   with tarragon vinegar (see page 163)
1 tablespoon chopped parsley

1. Heat the oven to 190°C/375°F/gas mark 5.
2. Trim the chicken livers, taking care to remove any greenish parts as they will be bitter.
3. Heat half the oil in a small roasting pan and add the unpeeled garlic cloves.

Roast in the oven for 15 minutes, but do not allow the garlic to brown. Remove from the oven and leave to infuse for a further 20 minutes. Strain through a fine sieve, reserving the oil. Peel the garlic cloves and mash the pulp until smooth.
4. Heat the garlic oil in a saucepan and cook the mushrooms, stirring frequently. Stir in the dried spices and cook for 2 minutes.
5. Remove the soaked ceps from their water with a slotted spoon. Drain and chop. Line a sieve with muslin or a clean J-cloth and strain the water to remove any grit. Add the ceps, the strained water and the thyme to the mushroom mixture. Cook, stirring frequently, until the mushrooms are soft and the liquid is syrupy. Add the garlic pulp. Remove from the heat and keep warm. Remove the sprig of thyme.
6. Heat the remaining oil in a large frying pan and fry the chicken livers until brown on the outside but still pink in the middle. Add the balsamic vinegar, scraping the bottom of the pan to pick up any sediment. Add the mushroom mixture and grapes. Taste and season with salt and pepper.
7. Toss the salad leaves in the French dressing and place on a serving dish. Pour the chicken liver and mushroom mixture on top, sprinkle with the chopped pecans and parsley, and serve.

 *WHITE RHÔNE/CLARET*

LAMBS' KIDNEYS WITH BUTTERNUT SQUASH AND RED PEPPERS

SERVES 4

PER PORTION Energy: 1353kj/322kcal
Fat: 11.0g Saturated fat: 2.3g

12 lambs' kidneys
2 tablespoons olive oil
1 Spanish onion, finely sliced
450g/1lb butternut squash, peeled and
*   chopped into 2.5cm/1 inch chunks*
1 tablespoon chopped fresh thyme
1 tablespoon cider vinegar
2.5cm/1 inch piece fresh ginger, grated
75ml/5 tablespoons medium sherry
2 large red peppers, deseeded, skinned
*   and diced*
2 tablespoons water (optional)
salt and freshly ground black pepper

To serve:
4 × 13cm/5 inch rounds granary bread,
*   toasted*
small bunch watercress

1. Skin the kidneys and cut them in half horizontally. Remove the cores with a pair of scissors and cut the kidneys into thin slices.
2. Heat half the oil in a large saucepan and sweat the onion until soft but not coloured. Add the squash, half the thyme, the vinegar, ginger and half the sherry. Cover and cook until the squash

is soft but still holding its shape, about 10–15 minutes. When tender, remove the lid and check the consistency of the liquid; reduce by boiling until syrupy, if necessary. Add the diced red peppers.
3. Heat the remaining oil in a frying pan, add the kidneys and sauté until brown on the outside and pink in the middle. Drain in a sieve over a bowl, discarding the juices as they can be bitter. Add the remaining sherry to the pan and reduce, by boiling rapidly, to a syrupy consistency; splash in 2 tablespoons water if required. Return the kidneys to the pan, add the remaining thyme and warm through. Season to taste with salt and pepper.
4. To serve: Spoon some warm squash and pepper mixture on to the warmed croûtes, place the kidneys on top and spoon over the juices. Garnish with watercress.

 *LIGHT RED*

PÂTÉS AND DIPS

PÂTÉS AND DIPS

FIELD MUSHROOM PÂTÉ

This is best made a day ahead to allow the flavours to develop.

SERVES 4

PER PORTION Energy: 753kj/179kcal
Fat: 6.5g Saturated fat: 1.0g

2 tablespoons olive oil
1 Spanish onion, finely chopped
30g/1oz dried ceps or porcini, soaked in
   150ml/¼ pint hot water for 30
   minutes
450g/1lb field mushrooms, finely
   chopped
110g/4oz brown-cap mushrooms
5 tablespoons Madeira
1 tablespoon chopped thyme
salt and freshly ground black pepper
250g/8–9oz quark, drained

1. Heat the olive oil in a large, heavy-bottomed saucepan and cook the onion until soft but not coloured.
2. Remove the soaked ceps or porcini from their water with a slotted spoon; drain and chop. Line a sieve with muslin or a clean J-cloth and strain the water to remove any grit. Reserve the liquid.

3. When the onions are soft, add all the mushrooms and the reserved liquid. Turn up the heat and cook, stirring frequently, until the mushrooms are soft.
4. Add the Madeira, thyme, salt and pepper, and reduce until the mixture is dry; this can take a while.
5. Pile the mixture into a food processor and process on the pulse button to break up; do not process too finely. Leave to cool.
6. When cool, stir in the drained quark. Season to taste with salt and pepper. Keep refrigerated.

 *LIGHT RED*

FRESH ASPARAGUS DIP

SERVES 4

PER PORTION Energy: 559kj/133kcal
Fat: 3.9g Saturated fat: 0.4g

900g/2lb fresh asparagus
1 tablespoon sunflower oil
1 Spanish onion, finely chopped
75ml/5 tablespoons dry white vermouth
150ml/¼ pint quark
salt and freshly ground black pepper

To serve:
Melba toast (see page 242)

1. Trim and wash the asparagus.
2. Heat the oil in a saucepan and cook the onions until soft but not coloured.
3. In a pan of boiling salted water, cook the asparagus until tender, about 6 minutes.
4. Drain the asparagus and refresh under cold water until cold. Dry, reserving 4 tips as garnish.
5. When the onions are soft, pour in the vermouth and boil until the juices are syrupy.
6. Place in a food processor with the asparagus and process until smooth. Push through a sieve.
7. If the mixture is watery, return to the rinsed-out saucepan and boil to reduce slightly; do not alter the colour by cooking too long, leave to cool.
8. When completely cold, stir in the quark. Taste and season with salt and pepper. Pour into a bowl and chill.

9. When ready to serve, garnish with the asparagus tips and serve with Melba toast.

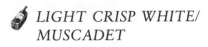 *LIGHT CRISP WHITE/ MUSCADET*

CELERIAC AND SUN-DRIED TOMATO DIP

SERVES 4

PER PORTION Energy: 485kj/115kcal
Fat: 3.8g Saturated fat: 0.4g

1 tablespoon olive oil
1 Spanish onion, finely chopped
450g/1lb celeriac
150ml/¼ pint chicken stock
75ml/5 tablespoons dry vermouth
½ teaspoon tomato purée
salt and freshly ground pepper
1 teaspoon lemon juice or cider vinegar
110g/4oz quark
4 dried sun-dried tomatoes, soaked in
*   hot water for 20 minutes, drained,*
*   and finely chopped*
1 tablespoon chopped flat-leaf parsley

To serve:
toasted brown bread

1. Heat the oil in a large saucepan and cook the onion until soft but not coloured.
2. Wash and peel the celeriac and cut into 1cm/½ inch chunks.
3. When the onions are tender, add the celeriac with the stock, vermouth and tomato purée and simmer for 20–30 minutes, until tender.
4. When soft, process the mixture until smooth. Season to taste with salt, pepper and lemon juice or vinegar. Leave to cool.
5. When cold, stir in the quark, sun-dried tomatoes and half the parsley.

Taste and season again if necessary. Transfer to a bowl and garnish with the remaining parsley. Serve with toast.

 *WHITE ALSACE*

FISH FIRST COURSES

FISH FIRST COURSES

PREPARATION FOR COOKING

REMOVING THE SCALES
Large fish have dry scales which should be removed before cooking. To do this, scrape a large knife the wrong way along the fish (from tail to head). This can be a messy business as the scales tend to fly about; it can be cleanly done in a plastic carrier bag to prevent this. However, unless you are buying fish from a wholesale market, the fishmonger will do it for you.

Remove the scales with the back of a knife.

GUTTING AND CLEANING
The fishmonger will probably clean the fish, but if you are to do it yourself, you will need a very sharp knife. Fish skin blunts knives faster than anything else. If the fish is to be stuffed or filleted, it does not matter how big a slit you make to remove the entrails. If it is to be left whole, the shorter the slit the better. Start just below the head and slit

through the soft belly skin. After pulling out the innards, wash the fish under cold water. If it is large and of the round type, make sure all the dark blood along the spinal column is removed. Now carefully cut away the gills. Take care not to cut off the head if you want to serve the fish whole. Otherwise, cut off the head and tail now. To remove the fins, cut the skin round them, take a good grip (if you salt your fingers well, it will stop them slipping) and yank sharply towards the head. This will pull the fin bones out with the fin.

Remove the innards and wash thoroughly.

SKINNING AND FILLETING FLAT FISH
Fish skin is easier to remove after cooking. But sometimes the fish must be skinned beforehand. Most whole fish are not skinned or filleted before grilling, but sole (and lemon sole, witch and plaice) are skinned on at least the dark side, and sometimes on both sides.

To do this, make a crosswise slit through the skin at the tail, and push a finger in. You will now be able to run the finger round the edge of the fish loosening the skin. When you have done this on both edges, salt your fingers to prevent slipping, take a firm grip of the skin at the tail end with one hand, and with the other hold the fish down. Give a quick, strong yank, peeling the skin back towards the head. If necessary, do the same to the other side.

Flat fish are generally filleted into four half-fillets. To do this, lay the fish on a board with the tail towards you. Cut through the flesh to the backbone along the length of the fish. Then, with a sharp, pliable knife, cut the left-hand fillet away from the bone, keeping the blade almost flat against the bones of the fish. Swivel the fish round so the head is towards you and cut away the second fillet in the same way. Turn the fish over and repeat the process on the other side. (If you are left-handed, tackle the right-hand fillet first.)

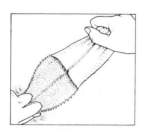

Remove the skin from a flat fish in one piece.

To fillet a flat fish, stroke the flesh away from the bones.

FILLETING AND SKINNING ROUND FISH

Round fish are filleted before skinning. If they are to be cooked whole, they are cooked with the skin, but this may be carefully peeled off after cooking, as in the case of a whole poached salmon. To fillet a round fish, lay it on a board and cut through the flesh down to the backbone from the head to the tail. Insert a sharp, pliable knife between the flesh and the bones and slice the fillet away from the bones, working with short strokes from the backbone and from the head end. Remember to keep the knife as flat as possible, and to keep it against the bones. When the fillet is almost off the fish you will need to cut through the belly skin to detach it completely. Very large round fish can be filleted in four, following the flat fish method, or the whole side can be lifted, as described here, and split in two once off the fish.

TO SKIN A FISH FILLET

Put it skin side down on a board. Hold the tip down firmly, using a good pinch of salt to help get a firm grip. With a sharp, heavy, straight knife, cut through the flesh, close to the tip, taking care not to go right through the skin. Hold the knife at right angles to the fish fillet, with the blade almost upright. With a gently sawing motion, work the flesh from the skin, pushing the fillet off rather than cutting it. The reason for keeping the knife almost upright is to lessen the danger of cutting through the skin, but with practice it is possible to flatten the knife slightly, so that the sharp edge is foremost, and simply slide it forward, without the sawing motion.

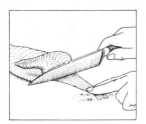

To skin a fillet, grip the tail with one hand and push the flesh off the fillet with a knife.

TO BONE SMALL FISH

Split the fish open completely, clean thoroughly and lay, skin side up, on a board. With the heel of your hand, press down firmly on the backbone of the fish. This will loosen it. Turn it over, cut through the backbone near the head and pull it out with all or nearly all, the sidebones attached to it. Remove any remaining bones with tweezers: this is known as pinboning.

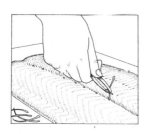

Remove the bones with tweezers or pliers.

TO DEVEIN PRAWNS

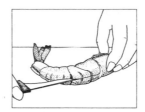

Using a sharp knife, make a small incision the length of the back of the prawn.

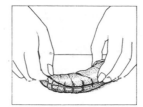

Carefully pull away the dark intestinal vein.

After preparing shellfish and other fish, to avoid retaining its odour on your hands, rinse first under running cold water, then wash thoroughly with detergent in hot water.

LIME-MARINATED SALMON WITH PAPAYA

SERVES 4

PER PORTION Energy: 1036kj/247kcal
Fat: 16.5g Saturated fat: 3.4g

*500g/1lb 2oz piece fresh salmon fillet,
    skinned (see page 88)*
1 tablespoon chopped fresh dill
salt and freshly ground black pepper
1 papaya
rocket leaves or watercress

For the marinade:
1 shallot, finely chopped
zest and juice of 1 lime
1 tablespoon good-quality olive oil
*1 fresh green chilli, finely chopped (see
    page 91)*

1. Remove any bones from the salmon and slice on the diagonal into 0.5cm/¼ inch thick slices. Lay the slices in a non-corrosive dish.
2. Mix the marinade ingredients with half the dill, pour over the fish and refrigerate for 2 hours, giving an occasional stir. It is ready as soon as it looks 'cooked' – opaque rather than glassy. (If the fish is really finely sliced, as little as 30 minutes will do; if thickly sliced, it can take more than 2 hours.)
3. When the fish is ready, season with salt and pepper.
4. Peel the papaya, remove the seeds and slice the flesh lengthwise into pieces slightly thicker than the salmon.
5. To serve: Arrange the salmon and papaya on a serving plate in overlapping slices. Spoon the marinade over and sprinkle with the remaining chopped dill. Garnish with rocket or watercress.

 *CHARDONNAY*

SWEET AND SOUR CEVICHE

SERVES 4

PER PORTION Energy: 514kj/122kcal
Fat: 4.5g Saturated fat: 0.9g

*450g/1lb fillet of monkfish, halibut or
  salmon, skinned and cut into thin
  slices or small strips (see page 88)*
2 tablespoons chopped fresh coriander
2 shallots or 1 red onion, sliced
zest and juice of 4 limes
1 tablespoon sesame oil
½ red chilli, finely chopped
2 tablespoons rice vinegar
1 tablespoon Thai fish sauce
1cm/½ inch fresh ginger, grated
*1 tablespoon preserved stem ginger,
  chopped*
salt and freshly ground black pepper

1. Put the fish and all the remaining
ingredients, except 1 tablespoon
coriander and the seasoning, into a
shallow dish and leave for 6 hours,
giving an occasional stir. (If the fish is
really finely sliced, less time will do.) It
is ready as soon as it looks 'cooked' –
opaque rather than glassy.
2. Season with salt and pepper. Arrange
on a serving dish and sprinkle liberally
with the remaining coriander.

 *GEWÜRTZTRAMINER/
CHABLIS*

CHILLIES
Take great care when preparing
chillies, as they contain a substance
which causes a burning sensation if it
comes into contact with the eyes, lips
or other sensitive parts of the skin.

The easiest way to avoid 'accidents'
is to use a fork to hold them in
position. Using a very sharp knife, cut
off the stalk end, cut the pod in half
lengthways, then scrape out and
discard the seeds. Slice or dice the
flesh and use as directed in the recipe.
Do remember to wash the chopping
board thoroughly afterwards.

SARDINE AND BUTTERBEAN SALAD

SERVES 4

PER PORTION Energy: 1093kj/260kcal
Fat: 12.4g Saturated fat: 2.4g

8 medium fresh sardines, scaled, gutted
and boned (see page 87–89)
5 tablespoons water
1 × 400g/14oz tin butterbeans, drained
and rinsed
2 garlic cloves, crushed
3 dried sun-dried tomatoes, soaked in
hot water for 20 minutes, drained and
shredded
1 red chilli (optional), finely chopped
(see page 91)
juice and zest 1 lemon
1 tablespoon chopped fresh basil
salt and freshly ground pepper
2 tablespoons good-quality olive oil

To serve:
rocket leaves
lemon wedges

1. Remove the back fin, head and tail
from each fish.
2. Put the water into a pan 15 minutes
before serving and bring to the boil. Add
the butterbeans and garlic. Reduce the
heat and simmer until the beans are
nearly falling apart, about 5 minutes.
Add the sun-dried tomatoes, chilli,
lemon zest, half the juice and half the
basil. Season to taste with a little salt and
pepper. Place on a warmed serving dish.

3. Heat the oil in a large frying pan over
a medium heat. Season the sardines
with salt and pepper and fry for about 2
minutes on each side. Drizzle with the
remaining lemon juice and basil.

Alternatively, heat the grill to its
highest setting, brush the sardines with
olive oil and grill, skin-side up, for
about 3 minutes. Baste with the lemon
juice and basil.
4. Serve immediately on the warm
butterbeans garnished with rocket and
lemon wedges.

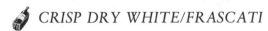 *CRISP DRY WHITE/FRASCATI*

WHITE FISH ROSTIS WITH SALSA VERDE

SERVES 4

PER PORTION Energy: 796kj/189kcal
Fat: 6.4g Saturated fat: 0.9g

These are called rostis (rather than fish cakes) because they include grated potato. This, plus the fact that they are low in fat, makes them lighter than conventional fish cakes. Beware that stray wisps of potato do not burn under the grill.

Orange roughy, imported from New Zealand, gets its name from its brilliant-coloured skin. The firm, dense flesh is pure white and tastes delicious, but can be substituted by cod, which may be easier to obtain.

340g/12oz orange roughy, or cod fillets,
  skinned (see page 88)
2 tablespoons sunflower oil
salt and freshly ground white pepper
2 tablespoons white wine
1 bay leaf
1 onion, chopped
225g/8oz cooked potato
1 tablespoon chopped coriander
1 tablespoon chopped parsley

To serve:
salsa verde (see page 159)
lime wedges

1. Set the oven to 200°C/400°F/gas mark 6.

2. Trim the fish fillets and remove any bones.
3. Lightly oil a large sheet of tin foil and place the fish on it. Season with salt and pepper, sprinkle with the white wine and add the bay leaf. Make a loose but tightly sealed parcel with the foil. Place on a baking sheet and bake in the oven for 12–15 minutes, or until cooked.
4. Meanwhile heat 1 tablespoon oil in a saucepan, add the onion and cook until soft but not coloured.
5. Grate the potato coarsely and put into a bowl.
6. Remove the fish from the foil, break into large flakes and add to the potato. Spoon the softened onions into the bowl, then stir in the coriander and parsley. Mix well and season to taste with salt and pepper. Shape the mixture into 4 patties and chill for 15 minutes.
7. Heat the grill to a medium setting.
8. Put the fish rostis on an oiled baking sheet, brush with the remaining oil and grill for 8 minutes, until golden and heated through. Serve immediately with a spoonful of salsa verde and a wedge of lime.

 *MEDIUM WHITE/SEMILLON*

SAUTÉ OF MONKFISH WITH PEAS AND LETTUCE

SERVES 4 as a first course; double the quantities of fish for a main course.

PER PORTION Energy: 693kj/165kcal Fat: 7.4g Saturated fat: 1.3g

*340g/12oz boned monkfish, skinned
  (see page 88–89)
2 tablespoons dry white vermouth
generous pinch ground cumin
generous pinch ground turmeric
2 tablespoons olive oil
1 onion, finely sliced
110g/4oz mangetout
110g/4oz frozen peas, cooked
½ tablespoon mixed chopped mint and
  parsley
caster sugar, to taste
salt and freshly ground white pepper
½ cos lettuce, shredded*

1. Slice the fish into 5cm/2 inch chunks. Place in a bowl and add half the vermouth, the ground cumin and turmeric. Stir, cover and refrigerate for 30 minutes.
2. Heat half the oil in a saucepan and cook the onion until soft but not coloured.
3. Add the mangetout and cook until nearly tender. Add the cooked peas, chopped herbs and remaining vermouth. Cook, stirring, until all the vegetables are soft. Taste and season with sugar, salt and pepper.
4. Heat the remaining oil in a frying pan or griddle and brown the monkfish on two sides. Reduce the heat and cook until all the fish is opaque. Remove from the pan and keep warm.
5. Stir the lettuce into the onion and pea mixture and cook until wilted.
6. To serve: Transfer the onion and pea mixture to a serving dish and arrange the sautéd fish on top.

 *MUSCADET DE SÈVRE ET MAINE*

SPICY PRAWN AND SQUID TAPAS

SERVES 4

PER PORTION Energy: 898kj/214kcal
Fat 7.5g Saturated fat 0.9g

450g/1lb squid, cleaned (see right)
150ml/¼ pint dry white wine
2 shallots, chopped
2 tablespoons chopped parsley
170g/6oz cooked prawns
2 teaspoons capers, rinsed and drained
2 tablespoons chopped parsley
1 tablespoon medium sherry

For the dressing:
2 tablespoons olive oil
2 teaspoons wine vinegar
¼ teaspoon dried mustard powder
large pinch crushed dried red chillies
pinch of salt
pinch of sugar

For the garnish:
red and yellow pepper strips

1. Drain the squid well and cut into rings.
2. Bring the wine to simering point, then add one chopped shallot and parsley. Add the squid and remove from the heat. Leave to stand until the squid is tender and looks opaque. Drain the squid in a sieve.
3. Mix the dressing ingredients together, then add the squid, prawns, capers, the remaining shallot, the parsley and

sherry. Mix well and place in a serving bowl. Garnish with red and yellow pepper and serve.

 WHITE RIOJA/ROSÉ/SPICY WHITE

PREPARING SQUID

Remove the blood (ink) and the entrails under cold running water – they will come out easily. Remove the clear plastic-like piece of cartilage that runs the length of the body on the inside.

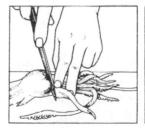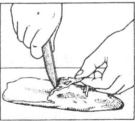

Cut off and throw away the head (it is the round middle bit with two large eyes). Scrape off the pinkish-purple outside skin – a fine membrane – from the body and the tentacles. Don't worry if you cannot get all the tentacles completely clear of it. Wash the body and tentacles to remove all traces of ink: you should now have a perfectly clean, white, empty squid.

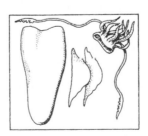 *Body, fins and tentacles.*

SPICY PRAWNS

SERVES 4

PER PORTION Energy: 711kj/170kcal
Fat 5.0g Saturated fat 0.5g

450g/1lb large uncooked prawns in
  their shells
2 tablespoons sunflower oil
2.5cm/1 inch fresh ginger, grated
1 garlic clove, crushed
1 green chilli, deseeded (see page 91)
1 teaspoon kalonji seeds (optional)
2 teaspoons whole cumin seeds
1 teaspoon sugar
1 tablespoon mustard seeds
½ teaspoon ground turmeric
55g/2oz fresh breadcrumbs
salt and freshly ground black pepper

1. Preheat the oven to 190°C/375°F/gas
mark 5.
2. Shell and devein the prawns (see page
89) and pile in a small, lightly oiled
ovenproof dish.
3. Place the ginger, garlic and chilli in
a spice mill and blend. Alternatively,
finely chop the ginger and chilli and
add the crushed garlic. Mix with the
kalonji, cumin, sugar, mustard seeds,
turmeric, breadcrumbs, salt and black
pepper.
4. Heat the remaining oil in a non-stick
frying pan, add the spice mixture and
cook over a low heat for 1–2 minutes,
stirring continuously.
5. Spoon the mixture on top of the
prawns and cover with foil. Bake for

25–30 minutes, or until the prawns are
cooked. Serve immediately.

 *AUSTRALIAN RIESLING*

PRAWN SALAD TIÈDE

SERVES 4 as a first course; double the prawn quantities for a main course.

PER PORTION Energy: 317kj/76kcal
Fat: 3.3g Saturated fat: 0.4g ·

8 'head-off' prawns, in their shells
2.5cm/1 inch piece fresh ginger, grated
½ green chilli, chopped (see page 91)
1 garlic clove, crushed
1 tablespoon soy sauce
1 tablespoon medium sherry
½ tablespoon balsamic vinegar
1 teaspoon Dijon mustard
1 tablespoon mango chutney
1 tablespoon sesame oil
110g/4oz sugarsnap peas
½ red pepper, sliced
110g/4oz baby corn
salt and freshly ground black pepper

To serve:
mixed salad leaves
toasted sesame seeds

1. Peel and devein the prawns (see page 89). Wash and pat dry, then place in a bowl and spread with the fresh ginger, chopped chilli and crushed garlic. Cover and refrigerate for at least 30 minutes, or overnight.
2. Mix together the soy sauce, sherry, vinegar, mustard and chutney. Set aside.
3. When ready to serve, put the salad leaves in a large bowl, or arrange on four side plates.
4. Heat the sesame oil in a wok or heavy-bottomed frying pan, add the prawns in a single layer and fry for about 1 minute. Remove from the pan with a slotted spoon. Reduce the heat.
5. Add the sugarsnap peas, red pepper, baby corn and soy sauce mixture and stir-fry until the vegetables are *al dente* and the sauce syrupy. Return the prawns to the pan, heat through, then taste and season with pepper, if necessary. Pile on to the salad leaves, stir lightly once and sprinkle with sesame seeds. Serve immediately.

 *LIGHT WHITE/PINOT GRIGIO*

FISH MAIN COURSES

FISH MAIN COURSES

STEAMED SQUID

SERVES 4

PER PORTION Energy: 996kj/237kcal
Fat 5.2g Saturated fat: 0.4g

1 leek, shredded
2 large carrots, shredded
1 × 2.5cm/1 inch piece fresh ginger, cut
   into shreds
1 small bunch chives, roughly chopped
salt and freshly ground black pepper
675g/1½lb small squid, cleaned (see
   page 95)

To serve:
red pepper sauce (see page 157)

1. Mix the leek, carrots, ginger and
chives together. Season with salt and
pepper and carefully stuff into the body
of the squid.
2. Place the squid in the top half of a
steamer and scatter with the tentacles
and any remaining stuffing. Steam for
15 minutes.
3. Pile on to a serving dish and serve
immediately. Hand the red pepper sauce
separately.

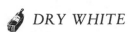 *DRY WHITE*

INDONESIAN FISH CURRY

SERVES 4

PER PORTION Energy: 1289kj/308kcal
Fat: 7.4g Saturated fat: 4.1g

Coconut is high in saturated fat, so use
sparingly in cooking.

*2 large potatoes, peeled and chopped
    into quarters*
675g/1½lb monkfish
juice of 1 lime
1 tablespoon sunflower oil
1 onion, chopped
*5cm/2 inch piece fresh root ginger,
    grated*
1 garlic clove, crushed
2 teaspoons ground coriander
2 teaspoons ground cumin
1 teaspoon ground turmeric
¼ teaspoon hot chilli seasoning
salt and freshly ground black pepper
230g/7½oz tin tomatoes
2 tablespoons coconut milk powder

1. Bring a large saucepan of salted water
to the boil and cook the potatoes for
15–20 minutes, or until tender. Drain.
2. Skin the fish, cut into 8cm/3 inch
pieces and sprinkle with the lime juice.
3. Heat the oil in a large saucepan and
cook the onion over a low heat for 10
minutes, or until nearly soft.
4. Add the ginger, garlic, spices, salt and
pepper and cook for another 2 minutes.
Add the tomatoes, coconut powder and
lime juice from the fish and simmer for
15 minutes.
5. Add the potatoes and fish and
simmer for a further 10 minutes, or
until the fish is cooked.

 *SPICY DRY WHITE*

ROAST HALIBUT WITH LENTILS

Fillets of halibut are better for this dish than halibut steaks. Puy lentils, which come from the Auvergne region of central France, are small and dark grey-green in colour. Brown or green lentils can be substituted, but need to be soaked in cold water for 4 hours before use.

SERVES 4

PER PORTION Energy: 1671kj/398kcal Fat: 8.6g Saturated fat: 0.9g

4 × 170g/6oz halibut fillets, unskinned
seasoned flour
sunflower oil

For the lentils:
2 large leeks, washed and sliced
4 tablespoons water
1 × 1.25cm/½ inch piece root ginger,
  peeled and cut into slivers
225g/8oz Puy lentils (or brown lentils,
  soaked for 4 hours)
salt and freshly ground black pepper
1 tablespoon chopped parsley
1 teaspoon chopped sage

For the garnish:
lemon wedges

1. Dip the fish, skin side only, into the seasoned flour and shake off any excess.
2. Preheat the oven to its highest setting.
3. Meanwhile, prepare the lentils. Put the leeks into a heavy saucepan with the water and ginger. Bring to the boil and allow all the water to evaporate. Leave the leeks over the heat and let them brown slowly.
4. Remove from the heat and add the drained lentils and enough water to just cover. Bring to the boil, season with salt and pepper, then simmer for 35 minutes.
5. When the lentils have been cooking for 30 minutes, start cooking the fish. Fry it, skin side only, in a little, very hot sunflower oil. Ideally, this should be done on a griddle or ridge-bottomed frying pan. Let it sizzle for 2 minutes. Turn the fish over into a roasting dish and cook in the oven for 3–4 minutes, depending on the thickness of the fillets.
6. Drain any excess liquid off the lentils, add the herbs and season to taste with salt and pepper.
7. Pile the lentils on to a warmed serving dish and arrange the halibut, skin side up, on top of the lentils. Garnish with the lemon wedges.

 *CHARDONNAY/ROSÉ*

SOLE BAKED IN SAUTERNES WITH FENNEL AND LOVAGE

SERVES 4

PER PORTION Energy: 838kj/199kcal
Fat: 5.8g Saturated fat: 1.1g

1 tablespoon olive oil
1 shallot, finely chopped
*1 head Florence fennel, cored and finely
    sliced (reserve the fronds/leaves)*
pinch of fennel seeds (optional)
grated zest and juice of 1 orange
*2 tablespoons chopped lovage or celery
    tops*
*3 medium sole, skinned and filleted (see
    page 87)*
*290ml/½ pint hot fish stock (see page
    153)*
100ml/3½fl oz Sauternes
salt and freshly ground white pepper

To serve:
fennel fronds, chopped

1. Set the oven to 180°C/350°F/gas
mark 4.
2. Heat the oil in a saucepan, add the
shallot, sliced fennel and fennel seeds (if
using) and cook slowly for 10 minutes,
or until the fennel is soft. Add the
orange juice and zest and lovage.
3. Put the mixture into the bottom of an
ovenproof dish. Fold the fish fillets into
neat parcels, skinned side inside.
Arrange on top of the vegetables. Pour

over the stock and Sauternes. Season
with salt and pepper. Cover with a lid
and bake in the oven for 10 minutes.
4. Lift the fillets on to a plate, strain the
fish liquid into a saucepan, place the
vegetables around the fish and keep
warm.
5. Reduce the fish liquid to 125ml/4fl
oz, or until syrupy, by boiling rapidly.
Taste and adjust seasoning, if necessary.
Pour over the vegetables and serve
immediately, sprinkled with chopped
lacy fennel fronds.

 *CHABLIS*

ROAST COD WITH GARLIC

This recipe is best made with narrow rather than wide fillets of fish.

SERVES 4

PER PORTION Energy: 831kj/198kcal
Fat: 5.6g Saturated fat: 0.8g

4 × 170g/6oz cod fillets, unskinned
salt and freshly ground black pepper
seasoned flour
150ml/¼ pint good-quality olive oil
4 garlic cloves, unpeeled

To serve:
lemon wedges

1. Preheat the oven to 200°C/400°F/gas mark 6.
2. Pinbone the cod fillets if necessary (see page 88). Season with salt and pepper and dip them, skin side down, into the seasoned flour. Shake off excess.
3. Heat the oil in a roasting tin. Add the garlic and bake in the oven for 15 minutes. Remove the tin from the oven and increase the oven temperature to its highest setting.
4. Set the oil in the tin over direct heat and add the cod, skin side down. Let it sizzle for 2 minutes.
5. Turn the cod skin side uppermost, and roast in the oven for 3 minutes or until cooked (it should be opaque and firm).

6. To serve: Place the cod, skin side uppermost, on a serving dish with the baked garlic and lemon wedges.

NOTE: If the oil is hot when the fish is cooked in it, the fish will not absorb it.

 *PINOT NOIR*

HONEY-ROAST SEA BASS WITH PICKLED GINGER

SERVES 4

PER PORTION Energy: 1795kj/427kcal
Fat: 17.8g Saturated fat: 3.0g

1.35kg/3lb sea bass cleaned and scaled
1 teaspoon roasted Sichuan
 peppercorns, crushed
2 tablespoons clear runny honey
1 tablespoon sunflower oil
salt

For the marinade:
2 tablespoons sesame oil
salt and pepper
2 tablespoons medium sherry
⅓ of the pickled ginger (see Note)
zest of 1 lime
1 garlic clove, crushed

For the lime and ginger sauce:
⅔ of the pickled ginger (see Note)
1 tablespoon sesame seeds, toasted
2 spring onions, sliced
juice of 1 lime

1. With a sharp knife cut 3 slashes into both sides of the fish. Rub the fish skin with the peppercorns and honey.
2. Mix the marinade ingredients together and pour over and inside the fish. Cover and refrigerate for 30 minutes.
3. Set the oven to 190°C/375°F/gas mark 5.

4. Brush a large piece of tin foil with the oil. Place the fish, with its marinade, on the foil. Season with salt, wrap loosely, securing the edges firmly, and place on a baking sheet. Bake for 30 minutes.
5. Meanwhile, mix together the pickled ginger, sesame seeds, spring onions and lime juice.
6. When the fish is cooked, remove it from the foil, place on a warmed serving dish, pour over any juice from the foil, and sprinkle with the ginger and lime mixture.

NOTE: To make pickled ginger, peel and slice very finely a 7½cm/3 inch piece of root ginger. Marinade in 2 tablespoons rice wine vinegar for 1 hour. Drain and use as required.

 *SAUVIGNON BLANC*

TROUT WITH CORIANDER AND MINT RELISH

Fish can be difficult to cook under a domestic grill: we recommend, if available, using a fish-holder or griddle.

SERVES 4

PER PORTION Energy: 836kj/200kcal
Fat: 9.3g Saturated fat: 3.3g

4 × 225g/8oz trout, cleaned
sunflower oil for brushing

For the relish:
30g/1oz fresh coriander
30g/1oz fresh mint
30g/1oz fresh coconut, grated
150ml/¼ pint low-fat natural yoghurt
juice of ½ lemon
2 teaspoons caster sugar
1 green chilli, deseeded (optional) (see
  page 91)
salt and freshly ground black pepper

1. Make the relish by blending all the ingredients in a food processor or liquidizer.
2. Heat the grill or barbecue.
3. Rinse the trout under cold water and dry with absorbent paper. Make 2–3 diagonal slashes in each side of the fish, nearly through to the bone. Brush the trout with oil and season with pepper.
4. Place the trout on a rack and grill for 5 minutes on each side until cooked (It

should be opaque and firm).
5. Lift the trout on to a serving plate and serve the relish separately.

 *SOAVE/FRASCATI*

STEAMED TROUT FILLETS IN LETTUCE

This recipe has been taken from *Easy to Entertain* by Patricia Lousada (Penguin London, 1990).

SERVES 4

PER PORTION Energy: 1175kj/280kcal
Fat: 11.2g Saturated fat: 2.4g

2 shallots, very finely chopped
1 tablespoon oil
170g/6oz mushrooms, finely chopped
squeeze of lemon juice
salt and freshly ground black pepper
8 large lettuce or cabbage leaves
4 large trout (pink-fleshed if possible),
*   filleted and skinned (see page 88–89)*

1. Sweat the shallots in the oil, stirring constantly. Add the mushrooms, lemon juice, salt and pepper. Sauté until the mushrooms give off their juices, then boil hard until all the juice has evaporated.
2. Blanch the lettuce in a large quantity of boiling salted water for 1–2 minutes, until just limp. Refresh in a bowl of cold water, then spread out on tea towels or absorbent paper to dry.
3. Trim and pinbone the trout fillets (see page 88–89). Pat the fillets dry and season with salt and pepper. Place a spoonful of the mushroom mixture on each fillet and roll up. Wrap in a lettuce leaf and place, seam down, in a steamer. Steam until tender, about 10 minutes.

 *DRY WHITE*

SALMON WITH GINGER AND ORANGE

SERVES 4

PER PORTION Energy: 1421kj/339kcal
Fat: 20.4g Saturated fat: 5.3g

4 × 170g/6oz salmon steaks
salt and freshly ground black pepper
4 pieces stem ginger
grated zest and juice of 1 orange
2 tablespoons syrup from stem ginger

1. Skin the salmon steaks. Place in a large bowl and sprinkle with salt and pepper.
2. Cut the stem ginger into fine julienne sticks and put into the bowl with the salmon. Add the orange zest.
3. Mix the orange juice with the ginger syrup and pour over the salmon. Cover and refrigerate for at least 1 hour.
4. Heat the grill to its highest setting.
5. Grill the salmon on one side until crisp. Turn over and baste with the orange and ginger mixture. Grill the second side for about 5 minutes or until golden brown. Serve.

 SPICY WHITE/CHILLED LIGHT RED/ROSÉ

CHICKEN, POULTRY
AND GAME

CHICKEN, POULTRY AND GAME

You may find the following information useful when preparing certain recipes in this book.

TRUSSING

The bird is trussed to keep it in a compact neat shape, usually after stuffing. Trussing large birds is unnecessary as the bird is to be carved up anyway, and trussing serves to prevent the inside thigh being cooked by the time the breast is ready. Small birds, especially game birds where underdone thighs are desirable, are trussed, but their feet are left on. Their feet may simply be tied together for the sake of neatness and the pinions skewered under the bird. They may also be trussed in a number of other ways, one of which is described below.

1. Arrange the bird so that the neck flap is folded over the neck hole, and the pinions turned under and tucked in tight. They will, if folded correctly, hold the neck flap in place, but if the bird is well stuffed the neck flap may have to be skewered or sewn in place.

2. Press the legs down and into the bird to force the breast into a plumped-up position. Thread a long trussing needle with thin string and push it through the wing joint, right through the body and out of the other wing joint.

3. Then push it through the body again, this time through the thighs. You should now be back on the side you started.

4. Tie the two ends together in a bow to make later removal quick.

5. Thread a shorter piece of string through the thin end of the two drumsticks and tie them together, winding the string around the parson's nose at the same time to close the vent. Sometimes a small slit is cut in the skin just below the end of the breastbone, and the parson's nose is pushed through it.

Small birds, such as quail, are invariably cooked whole, perhaps stuffed, and perhaps boned (see page 113). But medium-sized ones, such as chickens and guinea fowl, are often cut into two, four, six or eight pieces. Use a knife to cut through the flesh and poultry shears or scissors to cut the bones.

SPLITTING A BIRD IN HALF

Simply use a sharp knife to cut right through flesh and bone, just on one side of the breastbone. Open out the bird and cut through the other side, immediately next to the backbone. Then cut the backbone away from the half to which it remains attached. The knobbly end of the drumsticks and the fleshless tips to the pinions can be cut

111

off before or after cooking. In birds brought whole to the table they are left on.

JOINTING A BIRD INTO FOUR

First pull out any trussing strings, then pull the leg away from the body. With a sharp knife, cut through the skin joining the leg to the body, pull the leg away further and cut through more skin to free the leg. Bend the leg outwards and back, forcing the bone to come out of its socket close to the body. Turn the bird over, feel along the backbone to find the oyster (a soft pocket of flesh at the side of the backbone, near the middle). With the tip of the knife, cut this away from the carcass at the side nearest the backbone and furthest from the leg. Then turn the bird over again, and cut through the flesh, the knife going between the end of the thigh bone and the carcass, to take off the leg, bringing the oyster with it. Using poultry shears or a heavy knife, split the carcass along the breastbone. Cut through the ribs on each side to take off the fleshy portion of the breast, and with it the wing. Trim the joints neatly to remove scraps of untidy skin.

For six joints, proceed as above but split the legs into thigh portions and drumsticks. The exact join of the bones can easily be seen if the leg is laid on the board, skin side down. Cut through the fat line. With a cleaver, or the heel end of a knife, chop the feet off the drumsticks.

JOINTING INTO EIGHT

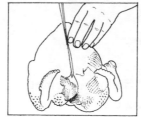 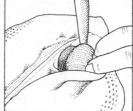

1. Turn the chicken over so the backbone is uppermost. Cut through to the bone along the line of the spine.
2. Where the thigh joins the backbone there is a fleshy 'oyster' on each side. Cut round them to loosen them from the carcass so that they come away when the legs are severed.

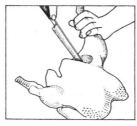 

3. Turn the bird over and pull a leg away from the body. Cut through the skin only, as far round the leg as possible, close to the body.
4. Pull the leg away from the body and twist it down so that the thigh bone pops out of its socket in the carcass and is exposed.
5. Cut the leg off, taking care to go between thigh bone and carcass and to bring the 'oyster' away with the leg. (Turn over briefly to check.) Repeat the process for the other leg.

 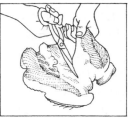

BONING

 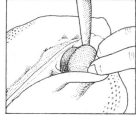

6. Carefully cut down each side of the breastbone to free the flesh a little.

7. Use scissors to cut through the small bone close to the breast. Cut away the breastbone.

8. Open up the bird. Cut each wing and breast off the carcass with scissors. Start at the tail end and cut to and through the wing bone near the neck.

1. Put the chicken breast side down on a board. Cut through to the backbone.

2. Feel for the fleshy 'oyster' at the top of each thigh and cut round it. Cut and scrape the flesh from the carcass with a sharp knife held as close as possible to the bone.

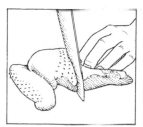 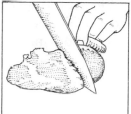

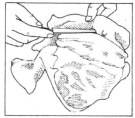 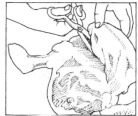

9. Cut the wing joint in two, leaving about one third of the breast attached to the wing.

10. Cut off the pinions from each wing. They can go into the stockpot with the carcass.

11. Separate the drumsticks and thighs, lay the legs skin side down on the board, and cut through where the thigh and lower leg bones meet, on the obvious fat line.

12. With a cleaver, or the heel end of a heavy knife, chop the feet off the drumsticks.

3. Continue along both sides of the backbone until the ribcage is exposed. At the joint of the thigh and pelvis, cut between the bones at the socket so that the legs stay attached to the flesh and skin, and not to the body carcass.

4. Keep working right round the bird, then use scissors to cut away most of the ribcage, leaving only the cartilaginous breastbone in the centre.

5. Using a heavy knife, cut through the foot joints to remove the knuckle end of the drumsticks.

6. Working from the inside thigh end, scrape one leg bone clean, pushing the flesh down towards the drumstick until you can free the thigh bone. Repeat on the other leg.

7. Working from the drumstick ends, scrape the lower leg bones clean in the same way and remove them. Remove as many tendons as possible from the legs as you work.

8. Now for the wings. Cut off the pinions with a heavy knife.

9. Scrape the wing bones clean as you did the leg bones.

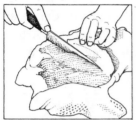 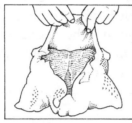

10. Carefully free the breastbone with the knife, working from the middle of the bird towards the tail.

11. Take great care not to puncture the skin, which has no flesh under it at this point so is easily torn.

12. You should now have a beautifully boned bird. Keep the neck flap of skin intact to fold over once the chicken is stuffed.

VENISON

Good deer meat should be dark red with a fine grain and firm white fat.

When preparing venison, remove as much of the membrane as possible. Venison is very low in fat, so it is often recommended that the meat be marinaded before cooking. If roasting it, the meat can be barded with bacon to help retain moisture.

For more information about red meat see page 133.

Roasting Tables

If using a fan (convection) oven, reduce the cooking times by 15 per cent, or lower the oven temperature by 20°C/40°F.

Poultry or game		Temperature			Cooking time	
		°C	°F	Gas	Per kg	Per lb
Chicken		200	400	6	35–45 mins	15–20 mins
NOTE: Few chickens, however small, will be cooked in much under an hour.						
Duck, goose						
	Small (under 2.5kg/5lb)	190	375	5	45 mins	20 mins
	Large (over 2.5kg/5lb)	180	350	4	55 mins	25 mins
Grouse		190	375	5	25–35 mins	
Guinea fowl		190	375	5	70 mins	
Partridge		190	375	5	20–25 mins	
Pheasant		190	375	5	45–60 mins	
Pigeon		200	400	6	25–35 mins	
Quail		180	350	4	20 mins	
Snipe		190	375	5	15–20 mins	
Teal		210	425	7	25 mins	
Turkey						
	Small (under 6kg/13lb)	200	400	6	25 mins	12 mins
	Large	180	350	4	35 mins	15 mins
NOTE: For more detailed timings see chart over. (Few turkeys, however small, will be cooked in under 2 hours.)						
Venison	Brown	220	425	7	15 mins	
	Roast	190	375	5	30 mins	10 mins
Wild duck		200	400	6	40 mins	
Woodcock		190	375	5	20–30 mins	

Thawing and cooking times for turkeys
Although the thawing times in this table can be relied on, the cooking times are
dependent on an accurate oven. For safety's sake, plan the timing so that, if all
goes right, the bird will be ready 1 hour before dinner. This will give you leeway
if necessary. To test if the turkey is cooked, press a skewer into the thickest part
of the thigh: the juices should run clear. When the bird is cooked, open the oven
door to cool the oven, then put the turkey on a serving dish and put it back in
the oven to keep warm.

Thawing in a warm room (over 18°C/65°F) or under warm water is not
recommended, as warmth will encourage the growth of micro-organisms, which
might result in food poisoning.

Weight of bird when ready for the oven, regardless of whether it is boned, stuffed or empty	Thawing time at room temperature 18°C/65°F	Thawing time in refrigerator 5°C/40°F	Cooking time at 200°C/400°F Gas mark 6	Cooking time at 180°C/350°F Gas mark 4
	hours	hours	hours	hours
4–5kg/8–10lb	20	65	2½–3 hours	
5–6kg/10–13lb	24	70	3–3¾ hours	
6–7kg/13–16lb	30	75	30 mins then	3¼–4
8–9kg/17–20lb	40	80	30 mins then	4–5
9–11kg/20–24lb	48	96	1 hour then	5–6

CHINESE CHICKEN SKEWERS WITH PAK-CHOI

SERVES 4

PER PORTION Energy: 1056kj/251kcal
Fat:10.2g Saturated fat: 2.3g

4 chicken breasts, skinned and boned
4 shallots, skinned and halved
110g/4oz shiitake mushrooms
450g/1lb pak-choi, washed, thick stems
   removed and chopped roughly
salt and freshly ground black pepper

For the marinade:
1 tablespoon soy sauce
1 tablespoon sesame seed oil
1 tablespoon rice wine or medium
   sherry
2 garlic cloves, crushed
1 tablespoon honey
1cm/½ inch piece fresh ginger, grated
5 cardamom pods, peeled, seeds crushed
½ fresh red chilli, finely chopped (see
   page 91)

For the garnish:
15ml/1 tablespoon sesame seeds,
   toasted
15ml/1 tablespoon chopped chives

1. Trim the chicken and cut into 2.5cm/
1 inch pieces. Put into a bowl with the
shallots. Mix all the marinade
ingredients together, pour over the
chicken, then cover and refrigerate
overnight.

2. Lift the chicken and shallots from the
marinade, pour the juices into a large
frying pan and reduce, by boiling
rapidly, until syrupy.
3. Heat the grill to a medium
temperature.
4. Thread the chicken, shallots and
shiitake mushrooms on to 8 skewers.
5. Place the chicken skewers under the
grill and cook for about 6 minutes on
each side until thoroughly cooked and
beginning to caramelize. Baste with
some of the marinade.
6. Meanwhile, add the pak-choi to the
remaining marinade and stir-fry until
just wilted. Taste and season with salt
and pepper. Remove from the pan and
transfer to a warm serving dish. Place
the skewers on top and sprinkle with
sesame seeds and chives. Serve
immediately.

 *GEWÜRZTRAMINER*

SAUTÉ OF CHICKEN WITH NECTARINES AND CHILLI

SERVES 4

PER PORTION Energy: 1295kj/308kcal
Fat: 10.0g Saturated fat: 3.0g

4 chicken breasts, skinned and boned
seasoned flour
½ teaspoon cumin
¼ teaspoon cayenne pepper
1 tablespoon sunflower oil
1 red chilli, finely chopped (see page 91)
2 nectarines, stoned and quartered (or
  tinned peaches, or dried peaches
  soaked in water)
5 tablespoons sweet sherry
2 tablespoons water
6 dried sun-dried tomatoes, soaked in
  hot water for 20 minutes, and
  chopped
1 tablespoon balsamic vinegar
30g/1oz feta cheese, crumbled
  (optional)
salt and freshly ground black pepper

For the garnish:
chopped coriander

1. Trim the chicken carefully and cut into bite-sized pieces. Toss in the seasoned flour with the cumin and cayenne pepper, then transfer to a plate in a single layer without touching.
2. Heat the oil in a large frying pan or wok and fry the chicken pieces, in batches if necessary, until golden brown and cooked through. Remove the chicken, then pour off any oil from the pan.
3. Put the chilli and nectarines into the pan with the sherry and 2 tablespoons of water. Bring to the boil and reduce, by boiling rapidly, to a syrupy consistency. Return the chicken to the pan and add the sun-dried tomatoes. Season to taste, add the vinegar and heat thoroughly. Pile into a warm serving dish, sprinkle with the cheese, if using, and chopped coriander.

 *RED LOIRE*

SAUTÉD LAPSANG CHICKEN WITH PEARS AND SHALLOTS

Earl Grey tea can be used instead of lapsang souchong.

SERVES 4

PER PORTION Energy: 1136kj/270kcal Fat: 10.5g Saturated fat: 2.3g

4 chicken breasts, skinned and boned
30g/1oz lapsang souchong tea, soaked
   in 200ml/7fl oz boiling water for
   1 hour
1 star anise
2 tablespoons sunflower oil
8 shallots, skinned and halved
8 garlic cloves
2 pears, peeled and sliced, or 8 dried
   pears, sliced
2 teaspoons green peppercorns, well
   rinsed
1 tablespoon calvados
salt and freshly ground black pepper

To serve:
mashed potatoes

1. Trim the chicken of any fat, then cut into 2.5cm/1 inch pieces. Put into a shallow dish.
2. When the tea is completely cold, strain it and pour over the chicken. Add the star anise, then cover and refrigerate overnight.
3. Strain the marinade and reserve. Discard the star anise.

4. Heat the oil in a large, heavy-bottomed frying pan, add half the chicken pieces and brown all over. Remove from the pan and brown the remaining chicken. Remove and keep warm.
5. Add the shallots, garlic and pears, and sauté until brown. Pour off any oil from the pan, then add the chicken to the mixture. Warm the calvados, add to the pan, light it with a match and shake the pan until the flames die down.
6. Add the green peppercorns and the reserved marinade liquid and continue cooking, stirring, for about 3 minutes or until the chicken is cooked.
7. Season to taste and serve with mashed potatoes.

 SPICY WHITE

CHICKEN BREASTS WITH PRUNES AND 'FRIED' ONIONS

SERVES 4

PER PORTION Energy: 998kj/238kcal
Fat: 5.1g Saturated fat: 1.6g

8 prunes, soaked overnight and stoned
4 chicken breasts, skinned and boned
salt and freshly ground black pepper
few drops balsamic vinegar
'fried' onions (see page 199)

For the garnish:
small bunch of watercress

1. Put 4 prune halves between the main part of the breast and the loose fillet of each piece of chicken. Season with salt, pepper and balsamic vinegar.
2. Wrap each breast in cling film. Place in a steamer and cook for 25 minutes.
3. Remove the chicken from the steamer, unwrap and place on a serving dish. Spoon over the prepared onions and garnish with watercress.

 *CLARET*

Sauté of Chicken with Nectarines and Chilli

Turkey and Parsnip Hotpot

Pot-roast Lemon Guinea Fowl with Chick Peas, Courgettes and Sun-dried Tomatoes

Pork Kebabs with Marinated Watercress

Black and White Pasta with Prawns

Spaghetti with Mussels

CHICKEN WITH PRUNES, OLIVES AND CAPERS

SERVES 4

PER PORTION Energy: 1572kj/374kcal
Fat: 13.7g Saturated fat: 3.3g

1 chicken, jointed and skinned (see page 112)
2 garlic cloves, crushed
2 tablespoons cider vinegar
2 tablespoons olive oil
1 tablespoon chopped fresh oregano
salt and freshly ground black pepper
12 prunes, stoned
12 green olives, stoned
4 tablespoons capers, drained and rinsed
2 tablespoons caster sugar
8 tablespoons dry white wine
2 teaspoons tomato purée
3 tablespoons water

1. In a large bowl combine the chicken with the garlic, vinegar, oil, oregano, salt, pepper, prunes, olives and capers. Cover and leave to marinate in the refrigerator for at least 2 hours.
2. Set the oven to 180°C/350°F/gas mark 4.
3. Arrange the chicken in a single layer in a large, shallow baking dish. Mix together the marinade, sugar, wine, tomato purée and water. Pour over the chicken.

4. Bake for 40–50 minutes, or until the chicken is tender, turning once.

 CLARET

SPICY CHICKEN

SERVES 4

PER PORTION Energy: 728kj/174kcal
Fat: 6.4g Saturated fat: 1.7g

4 chicken breasts, skinned

For the marinade:
150ml/¼ pint low fat natural
  yoghurt
2 garlic cloves, crushed
1 teaspoon garam masala
1 teaspoon ground cumin
1 teaspoon ground coriander
1 teaspoon paprika
½ teaspoon hot chilli seasoning
2 teaspoons sunflower oil
salt and freshly ground black pepper

To serve:
naan bread
brown rice (see page 191)
green salad

1. Prepare the chicken by cutting
diagonal slits about 5 mm/¼ inch deep
in the flesh.
2. Mix together all the marinade
ingredients in a large bowl. Add the
chicken and make sure it is well covered
with the marinade. Cover and
refrigerate for at least 1 hour.
3. Heat the grill or barbecue.
4. Cook the chicken for 15–20 minutes,
or until it feels firm to the touch,
turning halfway through the cooking.

Serve with naan bread, brown rice and
green salad.

 *CHARDONNAY/SPICY WHITE*

CITRUS-ROAST POUSSIN

SERVES 4

PER PORTION (without skin) Energy: 1979kj/471kcal Fat: 15.7g Saturated fat: 4.5g

4 × 450g/1lb poussins
1 tablespoon sunflower or hazlenut oil
zest and juice of 1 pink grapefruit
225g/8oz kumquats, halved
1 tablespoon clear runny honey
8 garlic cloves, skinned
2.5cm/1 inch piece fresh ginger, grated
100ml/3½fl oz white wine
1 sprig tarragon
salt and freshly ground black pepper

For the garnish:
small bunch of watercress
1 pink grapefruit, segmented without pith

1. Set the oven to 190°C/375°F/gas mark 5.
2. Clean the poussins and remove any hairs. Tie the legs together so that the poussins are 'trussed' (see page 111).
3. Heat the oil in a flameproof casserole. Add two poussins and brown all over. Remove from the casserole and brown the remaining two. Drain off and discard any oil.
4. Reduce the heat, return all the poussins to the dish, then add the grapefruit zest and juice, the kumquats, honey, garlic, ginger, wine and tarragon. Season with salt and pepper. Bring to the boil.
5. Cover and pot-roast for 20–25 minutes, or until all the juices run clear, rather than pink, when the thigh is pierced with a skewer.
6. When ready, remove the string from the poussins, then arrange them on a serving plate.
7. Skim off any fat from the casserole dish, then simmer the juices for a couple of minutes. Add the grapefruit segments. Season to taste and pour around the poussins. Garnish with the watercress and serve.

 *SAUVIGNON BLANC*

CHICKEN LASAGNE WITH RED PEPPER SAUCE

SERVES 6

PER PORTION Energy: 1705kj/406kcal
Fat: 14.4g Saturated fat: 3.4g

675g/1½lb lean chicken meat, skinned
2 tablespoons olive oil
2 onions, finely sliced
celery stalk, finely diced
1 garlic clove, crushed
pinch cayenne pepper
pinch cinnamon
75ml/5 tablespoons medium sherry
   (optional)
290ml/½ pint chicken stock (see page
   152)
sprig of thyme
salt and freshly ground black pepper
squeeze of lemon juice
½ quantity/egg pasta (see page 173, or
   Note)
1 tablespoon chopped fresh parsley
1 tablespoon grated Parmesan cheese
2 quantities red pepper sauce (see page
   157)

1. Pick over the chicken, removing any fat or gristle. Mince in a food processor.
2. Heat half the oil in a heavy-bottomed frying pan, add the minced chicken and brown well all over. Remove and set aside. Reduce the heat and deglaze the pan with water. Heat the remaining oil, add the onions and celery and cook until soft. Add the garlic, cayenne pepper and cinnamon, and cook, stirring for 1 minute.
3. Add the sherry (if using), stir well and bring slowly to the boil, stirring continuously. Add the browned chicken, stock and thyme, and season with salt and pepper. Simmer slowly for 10 minutes until the sauce is very thick and syrupy. Taste, season again if necessary, and add a little lemon juice and the chopped parsley. Remove the sprig of thyme. Set to one side.
4. Cut the pasta into eight strips 23cm/9 inches long and 10cm/4 inches wide, or the correct length for your dish. Allow to dry for 1 hour.
5. Set the oven to 190°C/375°F/gas mark 5.
6. Spread a layer of the chicken sauce over the bottom of an ovenproof dish. Arrange a layer of pasta on top of this, then spoon over a thin layer of red pepper sauce. Continue layering in this way, finishing with the red pepper sauce. Sprinkle with Parmesan.
7. Bake for 35–40 minutes, until bubbling and heated through.

NOTE: Dried pasta can be successfully used in this recipe. Follow the manufacturer's cooking instructions.

 *VIN DE PAYS/ROSÉ*

TURKEY AND PARSNIP HOTPOT

SERVES 4

PER PORTION Energy: 1306kj/311kcal
Fat: 9.4g Saturated fat: 1.3g

450g/1lb turkey breast, skinned and
*   boned*
2 tablespoons sunflower oil
1 Spanish onion, finely chopped
30g/1oz dried mushrooms, soaked in
*   150ml/¼ pint hot water for 30*
*   minutes*
225g/8oz wild mushrooms, e.g. shitake,
*   oyster or morels, sliced*
150ml/¼ pint chicken stock (see page
*   152)*
1 tablespoon chopped sage or thyme
salt and freshly ground black pepper
1 tablespoon seasoned flour
450g/1lb parsnips, peeled, finely sliced
*   and blanched*
extra oil for grilling (optional)

1. Trim off any fat from the turkey breast and cut into thin strips.
2. Heat half the oil in a large saucepan and cook the onion until soft but not coloured.
3. Heat the oven to 190°C/375°F/gas mark 5.
4. Remove the soaked mushrooms from their water with a slotted spoon, then drain and chop. Line a sieve with muslin or a clean J-cloth and strain the mushroom water to remove any grit. Reserve the liquid.

5. When the onions are soft, add the fresh and soaked mushrooms and cook for 3 minutes or until beginning to soften.
6. Add the stock and the reserved liquid, bring to the boil and cook until syrupy: there should be about 2 tablespoons of liquid left. Stir in the herbs, season with salt and pepper and remove from the heat.
7. Coat the turkey pieces lightly in the seasoned flour and transfer to a plate, making sure the pieces are not touching. Heat the remaining oil in a heavy-bottomed frying pan and cook the turkey in two batches until brown all over. Remove with a slotted spoon and add to the onion mixture. Stir well to coat the turkey meat with sauce. Transfer to an ovenproof dish or shallow casserole.
8. Layer the parsnips on top in overlapping rows, then season with salt and pepper. Bake, uncovered, in the oven for 20–25 minutes.
9. Heat the grill to its highest setting. When the hotpot is ready, grill fairly quickly until the top is browned and crisp.

 *RHÔNE RED*

POT-ROAST LEMON GUINEA FOWL WITH CHICK PEAS, COURGETTES AND SUN DRIED TOMATOES

SERVES 6

PER PORTION (without skin) Energy: 16.34kj/38.9kcal Fat: 16.3g Saturated fat: 4.4g

2 oven-ready guinea fowl
2 small lemons
8 garlic cloves, unpeeled
2 sprigs basil
salt and freshly ground black pepper
1 tablespoon olive oil
3 tablespoons dry white vermouth
340g/12oz courgettes, chopped into
  2.5cm/1 inch rings
8 dried sun-dried tomatoes, soaked in
  hot water for 20 minutes and halved
400g/14oz tin chick peas, rinsed and
  drained

For the garnish:
fresh basil

1. Heat the oven to 190°C/375°F/gas mark 5.
2. Grate the zest of 1 lemon. Prick both the lemons in a few places and put them whole inside the body cavity of each guinea fowl with 4 garlic cloves and a sprig of basil.
3. Tie the legs together to truss the guinea fowl and keep the neck cavities slightly sealed. This will help to retain the shape of the birds and preserve the lemon flavour. Season with salt and pepper.
4. Heat half the oil in a flameproof casserole. Add one of the guinea fowl and brown all over. Remove from the pan and set aside.
5. Wipe out the pan if necessary and brown the second guinea fowl in the same way. Drain off any oil. Return the first guinea fowl to the pan.
6. Sprinkle over the lemon zest and half the vermouth. Bring to the boil, cover and bake in the oven for 20 minutes.
7. Baste the guinea fowl, then add the courgettes and sun-dried tomatoes. Return to the oven and roast for a further 20 minutes.
8. Ten minutes before the end of the cooking time, add the chick peas and remaining vermouth.
9. When ready, remove the guinea fowl and joint them as you would a chicken (see page 112). Discard the lemons and basil, but set aside the garlic. Arrange the meat on a warm serving plate. Lift the vegetables from the casserole with a slotted spoon and arrange around the guinea fowl. Push the skins off all the garlic cloves and return to the casserole.
10. Add a splash of cold water to the casserole and skim off as much fat as possible.
11. Simmer the juices in the pan for a couple of minutes. Season to taste and strain into a gravy boat.
12. Garnish the guinea fowl with fresh basil and hand the gravy separately.

 *NEW ZEALAND CHARDONNAY*

PHEASANT WITH THREE ONIONS

SERVES 4

PER PORTION Energy: 1875kj/446kcal
Fat: 18.9g Saturated fat: 5.0g.

2 medium pheasants
2 tablespoons olive oil
1 Spanish onion, sliced
2 red onions, sliced
½ teaspoon ground cumin
1 teaspoon sugar
225g/8oz shallots, peeled
100 ml/3½fl oz whisky
2 strips pared orange zest
salt and freshly ground black pepper
1 tablespoon Dijon mustard

For the garnish:
fresh chopped parsley

1. Set the oven to 190°C/375°F/gas mark 5.
2. Wash and dry the pheasants.
3. Heat half the oil in a large, heavy casserole and cook the onions until soft but not coloured. Add the cumin and sugar, turn up the heat and cook, stirring, until a rich caramel colour. Do not allow to burn. Turn off the heat.
4. Meanwhile, heat the remaining oil in a frying pan and brown one pheasant on all sides. Remove and put on top of the onions.
5. Brown the second pheasant with the shallots and, when ready, put into the casserole with the onions and the first pheasant. Return the casserole to a low heat.
6. Heat the whisky and pour over the pheasants. Light with a match and shake the casserole until the flames die down. Add the orange zest, season with salt and pepper and bring to the boil. Cover and put in the oven for 30 minutes, or until the pheasants are cooked.
7. When ready, remove and joint the pheasants; keep warm.
8. Place the casserole over a high heat and boil the juices until 3–4 tablespoons remain, stirring all the time. Add the mustard. Taste and season again, if necessary.
9. Remove the casserole from the heat and discard the orange zest. Spoon the onion mixture around the pheasants, sprinkle with the parsley and serve.

 *PINOT NOIR*

PHEASANT WITH AUBERGINE AND PARSNIP COUSCOUS

To reduce the fat content the pheasants can be skinned before cooking.

SERVES 4–6

PER PORTION Energy: 3132kj/746kcal Fat: 25.0g Saturated fat: 0.5g

2 oven-ready pheasants
salt and freshly ground black pepper
285g/10oz pre-cooked couscous
1 large aubergine
1 garlic clove, unpeeled
2 parsnips, peeled
6 spring onions, sliced on the diagonal
2fl oz water or stock
2 tablespoons Marsala

For the dressing:
1 tablespoon sesame oil
1 tablespoon soy sauce
1 tablespoon balsamic vinegar
1 tablespoon runny honey
½ teaspoon sea salt
pinch cayenne pepper
1cm/½ inch piece fresh ginger, peeled
    and finely grated
grated zest of ½ lemon

1. Heat the oven to 200°C/400°F/gas mark 6.
2. Wipe the pheasants and remove any remaining feathers. Season them inside and out with salt and pepper.
3. Cover the couscous with 2.5cm/1 inch water and leave to soak for 15 minutes.
4. Wrap the aubergine in lightly oiled foil, place on a baking sheet and bake on a low shelf in the preheated oven for 40 minutes or until soft. Add the garlic after 15 minutes.
5. Put the pheasants into a roasting tin, pour 5mm/¼ inch water into the pan and roast for 40–50 minutes, basting frequently.
6. Drain the couscous, transfer to a sieve or colander lined with muslin and place over a saucepan of boiling water. Cover with foil and seal the edges well. Steam for 30 minutes, or follow manufacturer's instructions on packet.
7. Using a vegetable peeler or mandolin, pare off strips of the parsnip.
8. In a saucepan of boiling salted water, cook the parsnips for 30 seconds. Remove with a slotted spoon and drain on absorbent paper.
9. Mix together the dressing ingredients, then add the spring onions and parsnips.
10. Remove the aubergine and garlic from the oven. Peel and crush the garlic. Peel the aubergine, put the flesh into a clean cloth and squeeze dry to extract any bitter juices. Break the flesh up into pieces and add to the dressing.
11. When the pheasants are cooked, remove from the roasting tin, cover and keep warm.
12. Heat the parsnip and aubergine dressing gently in a saucepan. Add the couscous and mix well, breaking up any lumps.

13. Make the gravy: pour off any fat from the roasting tin, then place the tin over the heat and deglaze with 3 tablespoons water or stock. Reduce to a syrupy consistency by boiling rapidly. Add the Marsala and return to the boil. Taste and season if necessary.

14. To serve: Put the couscous on a warm serving platter, place the pheasants on top and pour over the gravy.

SHIRAZ/RHONE RED

BRAISED VENISON WITH PLUM AND RED ONION COMPOTE

SERVES 8

PER PORTION Energy: 2102kj/500kcal Fat: 12.7g Saturated fat: 4.1g

6lb/2.7kg haunch of venison
1 tablespoon sunflower oil
1 onion, sliced
225g/8oz carrots, sliced
2 celery stalks, sliced
1 piece orange zest
salt and freshly ground black pepper

For the marinade:
1 tablespoon Sichuan peppercorns
1 × 75cl bottle red wine
1 tablespoon sunflower oil
1 onion, sliced

For the compote:
1 tablespoon oil
1lb/450g red onions, finely sliced
1 cooking apple, roughly chopped
450g/1lb red plums, halved and stoned
2 tablespoons cider vinegar

1. Trim the venison of any skin and membrane.
2. Toast the peppercorns in a dry frying pan until the pan is hot and the peppercorns begin to release their aroma.
3. Place the venison in a large earthenware or plastic bowl and add the peppercorns and the other marinade ingredients. Cover and refrigerate for 2–3 days, turning the meat occasionally.
4. Preheat the oven to 150°C/300°F/gas mark 2.
5. Remove the venison from the marinade, reserving the liquid. Heat the oil in a large, flameproof casserole and brown the venison well on all sides. Remove from the casserole.
6. Add the onion, carrots and celery and fry until lightly browned. Place the venison on top of the vegetables and strain the marinade over it. Add the orange zest.
7. Bring to simmering point, cover tightly and braise for 1½ hours.
8. Meanwhile, make the compote. Heat the oil in a heavy, flameproof casserole. Add the red onions and sweat, covered, on a low heat for about 30 minutes or until completely soft. Add the apple, plums and cider vinegar and simmer, uncovered, until the plums are soft, but still holding their shape. The compote should be thick; if it is not, strain the mixture into a saucepan and boil to reduce the liquid to a thick consistency. Return the fruit to the saucepan and heat gently.
9. When the venison is cooked, lift it out of the casserole and keep warm. Strain the liquid from the vegetables into a saucepan. Boil to reduce the sauce to a syrupy consistency. Season to taste.
10. Carve the meat and hand the compote and sauce separately.

 *CABERNET SAUVIGNON*

MEAT

MEAT

The younger the animal, and the less exercise it has taken, the more tender its meat will be, but its flavour will be less pronounced. For example a week-old calf will be as tender as margarine, and about as flavourless. An ox that has pulled a cart all its long life will be quite the reverse – good on flavour, but tough as old boots. A relatively young and therefore tender animal will have white or pale fat, rather than yellow; the meat will be less dark and the bones more pliable than in an older, tougher animal. So rump steak with a bright red hue and white fat may well be more tender than the dark flesh and yellow fat of older meat, but it will probably lose in flavour what it gains in texture.

BEEF

As tenderness is rated highly today, the most expensive cuts of meat are those from the parts of the animal's body that have had little or no exercise. For example, the leg, neck and shoulder cuts of beef are tougher (and therefore cheaper) than those taken from the rump or loin.

But apart from the age of the animal, there are other factors that affect tenderness. Meat must not be cooked while the muscle fibres are taut due to rigor mortis, which can last, depending on the temperature at which the carcass is stored, for a day or two. The state of the animal prior to slaughter can also affect the tenderness of the meat; for example, if it is relaxed and peaceful, the meat is likely to be more tender. Injections of certain enzymes (proteins that produce changes in the meat without themselves being changed) given to the animal before slaughter will produce the same result artificially.

But the most crucial factor affecting tenderness is the length of time that meat is stored before cooking. If hung in temperatures of 2°C/35°F, it will, due to enzyme activity, become increasingly tender. Temperatures should not be higher than this because although the enzyme activity would be greater, the risk of spoilage due to bacterial action would become high. For beef, 7 days is the minimum hanging time, while 3 weeks or a month are more desirable. However, with the commercial demands for quick turnover, the weight-loss during storage and the expense of storing, good hanging is rare these days. Some enzyme activity continues if the meat is frozen, and the formation and subsequent melting of ice-crystals (which, in expanding, bruise the fibres of the meat) means that freezing meat can be said to tenderize it. However, the inevitable loss of juices from the meat (and subsequent risk of dryness after cooking) is a disadvantage that outweighs the minimal tenderizing effect.

Hanging is most important in beef, as the animals are comparatively old, perhaps 2 or 3 years, when killed. It is less important for carcasses of young animals, such as calves and lambs, as their meat is relatively tender anyway.

Because, inevitably, some bacterial action (as well as enzyme action) must take place during hanging, the flavour of well-hung meat is stronger, or gamier, than that of under-hung meat. The colour will also deepen and become duller with hanging. But the prime reason for hanging meat is to tenderize it, rather than to increase or change its flavour. This is not so with game, including venison, which is hung as much to produce a gamey flavour as to tenderize the meat.

The last, and probably most important, factor that affects the ultimate tenderness of meat is the method of cooking. Half-cooked or rare meat will be tender simply because its fibres have not been changed by heat, and will still retain the softness of raw meat. But as the heat penetrates the whole piece of meat the fibres set rigidly and the juices cease to run. Once the whole piece of meat is heated thoroughly, all the softness of raw meat is lost and it is at its toughest. This explains the natural reluctance of chefs to serve well-done steaks – it is almost impossible to produce a tender well-done grilled steak.

But, paradoxically, further cooking (though not fast grilling or frying) will tenderize that tough steak. This is seen in stewing, when long, slow cooking gradually softens the flesh. A joint from an older animal, which has done much muscular work during its lifetime and is coarse-grained and fibrous, can be made particularly tender by prolonged gentle cooking. This is because much of the connective tissue present in such a joint, if subjected to a steady temperature of, say, 100°C/200°F, will convert to gelatine, producing a soft, almost sticky tenderness.

Joints with finer graining and little connective tissue, such as rump or sirloin, will never become gelatinous, and are consequently seldom cooked other than by roasting or grilling, when their inherent tenderness (from a life of inaction) is relied on. But they will never be as tender as the slow-cooked shin or oxtail, which can be cut with a spoon.

It does not matter that few people have any idea which part of the animal their meat comes from. But it is useful to know, if not how to do the butcher's job, at least which cuts are likely to be tender, expensive, good for stewing, or not worth having, and what to look for in a piece of meat.

VEAL

The cuts of veal, and their names, more closely resemble those of a lamb or sheep than those of grown-up beef.

As veal is more tender than beef, more of the animal is suitable for quick cooking (roasting, frying). But as there is little fat on a calf, care must be taken to moisten the meat frequently during cooking to prevent dryness. Owing to the absence of fat, veal is seldom grilled.

Most Dutch veal is milk-fed and intensively reared. It has a pale pink colour and some cuts are exceptionally tender. The taste, however, is mild to the point of insipidity, so it needs good seasoning – usually plenty of lemon, pepper or a good sauce. English veal and naturally reared veal is generally cheaper, has more flavour, and has a slightly more reddish hue. This is because the animals are older when killed than the Dutch intensively reared veal, and are generally, though not always, grass-fed. Veal should never look bloody or really red.

LAMB AND MUTTON

Animals weighing more than 36 kg/80lb are graded as mutton. Real mutton is seldom available in butchers' shops since all the animals are killed young enough to be called lamb. But there is a difference between the small sweet joints of the new season's spring lamb, and the larger lambs killed later in the year.

Really baby lambs, killed while still milk-fed, are extremely expensive, with very pale, tender flesh. A leg from such a lamb would feed only 2 or perhaps 3 people at most.

British lamb is very fine in flavour, but good imported New Zealand lamb is usually cheaper. As a general rule, New Zealand lamb joints come from smaller animals than the full-grown English lambs, but it should be remembered that 3 grades of New Zealand lamb are imported into Britain, ranging from excellent to very tough. All New Zealand lamb comes into the country frozen, so it stands to reason that some lambs have been more recently killed than others. The best time to buy New Zealand lamb is from Christmas through to the summer months.

Lamb should be brownish-pink rather than grey in colour, but not bloody. Because the animal is killed young, almost all the cuts are tender enough for grilling, frying or roasting, but the fattier, cheaper cuts are used for casseroles and stews too.

PORK

Pork used to be eaten mainly in winter, or as bacon, because of the difficulty of keeping it fresh. But with modern methods of refrigeration, pork is now eaten all year round.

The flesh should be pale pink, not red or bloody. Pork killed for the fresh meat market is generally very young and tender, carrying little fat.

BACON

Bacon pigs are killed when heavier than pigs destined for the fresh pork market, so the comparable cuts of bacon should contain more fat than those of fresh pork.

Since good refrigeration is now widely available, pork need no longer be salted as a preservative measure. Today pork is turned into bacon mainly for the flavour. Smoked bacon keeps slightly longer than green (unsmoked) but, again, modern smoking is done more for the flavour than for preservation.

Commercially produced bacon is generally mild. Bacon cured at home, without chemical preservatives, vacuum packs, etc., is likely to have more flavour and saltiness, but needs soaking before cooking.

Smoked and green bacon flesh look similarly reddish-pink. It should not be dry, hard, dark or patchy in colour. Smoked rind is yellowish-brown; green bacon rind is white.

English bacons vary according to manufacturer and price, some being saltier than others, so care should be taken if boiling without prior soaking. It is wise to soak large pieces to be cooked whole, such as gammons or forelocks. Smaller cuts, steaks and rashers, rarely need soaking.

Danish pigs are all cured in the same manner, giving a good quality, mild-tasting, not very salty bacon.

Roasting Tables

All joints of meat should be browned quickly at a high temperature in order to seal in the juices. They are then roasted at a lower temperature for the relevant number of minutes per kilogram or pound.

If using a fan (convection) oven, reduce the cooking times by 15 per cent, or lower the oven temperature by 20°C/40°F.

Meat		Temperature			Cooking time	
		°C	°F	Gas	per kg	per lb
Beef	Brown	220	425	7	15 mins +	
	Rare roast	160	325	3	35 mins	15 mins
	Medium roast				45 mins	20 mins
Lamb	Brown	220	425	7	15 mins +	
	Roast	190	375	5	55 mins	15 mins
Pork	Roast	200	400	6	65 mins	25 mins
Veal	Brown	220	425	7	20 mins +	
	Roast	180	350	4	55 mins	25 mins

BEEF DHANSAK

SERVES 4

PER PORTION Energy: 1598kj/382kcal
Fat: 10.9g Saturated fat: 3.0g

2 tablespoons sunflower oil
1 onion, chopped
2 garlic cloves crushed
450g/1lb lean braising steak, cut into 4
  mm/1½ inch chunks
1 green chilli, deseeded and sliced (see
  page 91)
1½ teaspoons ground cumin
1½ teaspoons ground coriander
1 teaspoon garam masala
4 green cardamoms, crushed
1 teaspoon ground turmeric
salt and freshly ground black pepper
170g/6oz split red lentils
5 tomatoes, skinned, deseeded and
  chopped
290ml/½ pint water
225g/8oz frozen leaf spinach, defrosted
  and drained
4 tablespoons chopped fresh coriander
2 tablespoons chopped fresh mint

1. Heat half the oil in a large, ovenproof casserole and cook the onion over a medium heat until golden and translucent. Add the garlic and cook for a further 2 minutes. Remove from the casserole with a slotted spoon and set aside.
2. Preheat the oven to 170°C/325°F/gas mark 3.
3. Add the beef to the casserole and brown evenly over a medium heat. Remove from the casserole with a slotted spoon and set aside with the onion and garlic. Pour a little of the water into the casserole and swirl it about, scraping any sediment stuck to the bottom; pour over the meat. Heat the remaining oil and add the chilli, cumin, ground coriander, garam masala, cardamoms, turmeric, salt and pepper and cook for 2–3 minutes.
4. Return the onion, garlic and meat to the casserole, then add the lentils, tomatoes and remaining water and bring to the boil. Cover and place in the oven and cook for 1½–2 hours.
5. Add the spinach, fresh coriander and mint, cook for a further 30 minutes, then serve.

 *BEAUJOLAIS VILLAGES*

STIR-FRIED BEEF JAPANESE-STYLE WITH GINGER AND ORANGE GLAZE

This recipe calls for Japanese soy sauce; if it is not available, light soy sauce is the best substitute. If you cannot obtain mirin (Japanese rice wine), light muscovado sugar or a sweet sherry can be used instead.

SERVES 4

PER PORTION Energy: 1443kj/344kcal
Fat: 15.8g Saturated fat: 4.2g

675g/1½lb lean beef (sirloin or rump)
2 tablespoons sunflower oil
140g/5oz French beans trimmed
110g/4oz carrots, cut into julienne strips
salt and freshly ground black pepper
1 tablespoon sesame seeds, toasted

For the marinade:
2 tablespoons Japanese soy sauce
2 tablespoons port
2 tablespoons mirin
grated zest and juice of 1 orange
1 dried chilli
1 tablespoon honey
1 tablespoon orange flower water
2.5cm/1 inch fresh ginger, grated

1. Place all the marinade ingredients in a small saucepan. Bring slowly to the boil, then simmer for 3 minutes, or until syrupy. Remove from the heat and leave to cool.

2. Slice the beef across the grain into thread-like strips 7.5cm/3 inches long. Place in a bowl with the marinade, then cover and refrigerate overnight.
3. Lift the beef from the marinade with a slotted spoon. Strain and reserve the marinade.
4. Heat half the oil in a wok, add the beans and marinade and cook for 2 minutes. Remove and keep warm.
5. Heat the remaining oil in the wok. Add half the beef, increase the heat and stir-fry until cooked but tender, about 2 minutes. Remove, keep warm and cook the remaining beef in the same way.
6. Return all the beef plus the beans and carrots to the wok and cook until hot and the juices are syrupy. Season to taste. Pile on to a warmed serving dish, scatter with sesame seeds and serve.

 *LIGHT RED*

VEAL MEATBALLS

SERVES 4

PER PORTION Energy: 773kj/184kcal
Fat: 5.7g Saturated fat: 1.8g

450g/1lb very lean veal, finely minced
4 large spring onions, chopped
2.5cm/1 inch piece fresh ginger, finely
   chopped
1 garlic clove, crushed
1 small green chilli, deseeded and finely
   chopped (see page 91)
2 tablespoons soy sauce
1 tablespoon wine vinegar
½ teaspoon ground, roasted Szechuan
   peppercorns
1 egg, lightly beaten
570ml/1 pint chicken stock (see page
   152)

For the sauce:
150ml/¼ pint low-fat natural yoghurt
1 teaspoon sesame oil
dash of Tabasco

For the garnish:
small bunch of watercress

1. Mix together the veal, spring onions,
ginger, garlic, chilli, soy sauce, vinegar
and peppercorns. Taste and season if
required. Add the egg and beat well.
2. With wet hands, shape the mixture
into balls the size of ping-pong balls and
place in the top half of a steamer (on a
plate if the holes are large). Put the
stock in the bottom half of the steamer.

Bring to the boil and steam the balls for
20 minutes.
3. Meanwhile, mix all the sauce
ingredients together and pour into a
small dish.
4. Serve the balls on a warm plate,
garnished with sprigs of watercress.
Hand the sauce separately.

 *LIGHT RED/CHIANTI*

CHINESE-STYLE LAMB WITH MUSHROOMS AND SMOKED OYSTERS

SERVES 4

PER PORTION Energy 1547kj/368kcal
Fat: 17.3g Saturated fat: 5.8g

*2 large lamb fillets from the best end of
    neck*
*1 tablespoon Chinese five-spice powder,
    dry roasted*
2 garlic cloves, crushed
2 tablespoons light soy sauce
salt and freshly ground black pepper
1 tablespoon sunflower oil
*225g/8oz oyster mushrooms, cut into
    strips*
*1.35kg/4½lb spinach, washed and
    chopped*
*1 × 110g/4oz tin smoked oysters,
    drained*
2 tablespoons rice wine or sherry
*290 ml/½ pint brown stock (see page
    151)*

1. Trim the lamb of any fat or gristle.
Rub the meat with the five-spice
powder and garlic. Place in a bowl,
pour over the soy sauce and season with
black pepper. Cover and refrigerate for
at least 30 minutes or overnight.
2. Set the oven to 240°C/475°F/gas
mark 8.
3. Remove the lamb fillets from the
bowl, reserving the marinade. Heat half

the oil in a heavy-bottomed frying pan
and brown the meat quickly on all
sides. Transfer to a roasting tin and
place in the oven for 8–10 minutes. The
lamb should still be pink in the centre.
4. Meanwhile, heat the remaining oil in
a wok or large frying pan, add the
mushrooms and cook for 2 minutes,
stirring constantly. Add the spinach to
the pan and cook until wilted. Add the
smoked oysters and rice wine and cook,
stirring, until warmed through.
5. Take the fillet out of the oven and
leave to rest in a warm place for 5
minutes.
6. Discard any fat from the roasting
pan, then pour in the marinade and
stock. Bring to the boil, stirring
continuously with a wooden spoon and
scraping the bottom of the pan to
loosen any sediment. Reduce the liquid,
by boiling rapidly, until syrupy. Taste
and season. Strain the juices into a
warmed gravy boat.
7. Slice the lamb on the diagonal and
serve with the warm mushroom and
spinach mixture.

 *SPICY RED/RHÔNE*

LAMB CASSEROLE

SERVES 4

PER PORTION Energy: 2105kj/501kcal
Fat: 22.9g Saturated fat: 9.8g

900g/2lb lean lamb, preferably leg
1 tablespoon oil
150ml/¼ pint brown stock (see page
* 151)*
sprig of basil
55g/2oz flour (for the huff paste)
salt and freshly ground black pepper

For the marinade:
150ml/¼ pint dry white vermouth
2 garlic cloves, crushed
1 large onion, sliced
1 celery stalk, chopped
sprig of rosemary
1 strip pared lemon zest

To serve:
basil and parsley gremolata (see page
* 162)*

1. Trim the lamb, cut into 5cm/2 inch pieces and put into a bowl.
2. Mix all the marinade ingredients together, pour over the lamb, then cover and refrigerate overnight.
3. Set the oven to 170°C/325°F/gas mark 3.
4. Remove the meat from the bowl. Strain the marinade, reserving it separately from the onions and garlic.
5. Heat the oil in a heavy-bottomed frying pan and brown the onions and garlic. Lift out with a slotted spoon and place in a casserole dish.
6. Brown the meat in the same pan, a few pieces at a time, adding more oil if necessary. Lay the browned meat on top of the onions. Deglaze the pan with water.
7. Pour the marinade into the empty pan. Add the stock and bring to the boil, scraping the bottom of the pan to loosen any sediment. Pour the liquid over the meat and add the sprig of basil. Season with salt and pepper.
8. Make a stiff dough by kneading water into the flour. Cover the casserole, then press a band of dough around it to seal the lid and dish completely.
9. Cook in the oven for 2 hours. Remove the rough and lid, transfer the meat and onions to a serving dish and keep warm. Discard the sprig of basil.
10. Boil the sauce rapidly to reduce to a syrupy consistency. Taste and season with salt and pepper, than pour over the meat. Serve sprinkled with the basil and parsley gremolata.

 *RIOJA/PINOT NOIR*

SPICY SHEPHERD'S PIE

SERVES 4

PER PORTION Energy: 1718kj/409kcal
Fat: 10.6g Saturated fat: 3.6g

2 teaspoons sunflower oil
2 onions, finely chopped
½ red pepper, finely chopped
2 carrots, finely chopped
675g/1½lb lean minced beef
2 teaspoons flour
2 teaspoons ground cumin
2 teaspoons ground coriander
½ teaspoons ground turmeric
½ teaspoon hot chilli seasoning
290ml/½ pint brown stock (see page
    151)
1 tablespoon tomato purée
salt and freshly ground black pepper

For the topping:
675g/1½lb mashed potatoes, made with
    semi-skimmed milk (see page 195)

1. Heat the oil in a large frying pan and
fry the vegetables for 5 minutes, or until
nearly soft and tender. Transfer to a
large saucepan.
2. Brown half the mince in the frying
pan, then transfer to the saucepan with
a perforated spoon. Brown the
remaining mince. Add the flour and
spices and cook for 30 seconds.
3. Add the beef stock and slowly bring
to the boil, stirring continuously. Now
add the tomato purée, salt and pepper.
Place in the saucepan with the

vegetables and mince mixture. Simmer
over a low heat for 45 minutes. The
final mixture should be moist but not
runny. Add extra water if necessary.
4. Preheat the oven to 200°C/400°F/gas
mark 6.
5. Pile the meat mixture into a casserole
dish. When cool, spread the mashed
potato over the top. Fork it up to leave
a rough surface, then place in the oven
and bake for 30 minutes.

 *SPICY RED/CROZES-
HERMITAGE*

MOROCCAN LAMB

SERVES 4

PER PORTION Energy: 1920kj/459kcal
Fat: 17.2g Saturated fat: 6.5g

675g/1½ lean leg of lamb
1 tablespoon olive oil
1 tablespoon ground cumin
2 teaspoons paprika
¼ teaspoon hot chilli powder
2 onions, sliced
2 garlic cloves, crushed
200ml/7fl oz water
2 tablespoons chopped fresh coriander
2 tablespoons chopped fresh parsley
110g/4oz raisins
salt and freshly ground black pepper

To serve:
boiled rice
green salad

1. Place the lamb with the oil, cumin, paprika, chilli powder, onions, garlic and 4 tablespoons of the water in an earthenware casserole dish; cover and refrigerate for at least 2 hours.
2. Preheat the oven to 160°C/325°F/gas mark 3.
3. Add the remaining ingredients to the casserole and cook in the oven for 2–2½ hours, or until tender. Serve with plenty of rice and salad.

 *RHÔNE RED*

PORK GOULASH

SERVES 4

PER PORTION Energy: 1347kj/321kcal
Fat: 15.8g Saturated fat: 4.8g

4 teaspoons sunflower oil
2 onions, finely chopped
1 large green pepper, deseeded and
    chopped
675g/1½lb shoulder of pork
1 tablespoon paprika
2 tablespoons tomato purée
150 ml/¼ pint vegetable stock (see page
    154)
salt and freshly ground black pepper
bouquet garni of 1 parsley sprig, 1
    thyme sprig, 1 celery stalk and 1 bay
    leaf, tied together with string

To serve:
low-fat natural yoghurt

1. Heat half the oil in a large, ovenproof
casserole, add the onion and pepper,
cover with a well-fitting lid and cook on
a gentle heat for 10–15 minutes without
browning.
2. Trim the pork of any fat, then cut the
meat into 2.5cm/1 inch cubes. Heat the
remaining oil in a large, non-stick frying
pan and brown the meat. Add the meat
to the onion mixture. Deglaze the pan
with a little water, scraping up any
sediment stuck to the bottom; pour over
the onion and meat mixture.
3. Heat the oven to 170°C/325°F/gas
mark 3.

4. Sprinkle the onion and meat mixture
with the paprika and cook gently over a
low heat for 2 minutes. Add the tomato
purée, stock, salt, pepper and bouquet
garni and bring to the boil. Cover with
a lid and place in the oven. Cook for
1½–2 hours until tender. Serve with
yoghurt.

 *RIOJA/BEAUJOLAIS*

PORK KEBABS WITH MARINATED WATERCRESS

SERVES 4

PER PORTION Energy: 1598kj/380kcal
Fat: 19.9g Saturated fat: 5.3g

*675g/1½lb lean pork, cut into 3cm/1½
    inch cubes*

For the marinade:
150ml/¼ pint low-fat natural yoghurt
1 garlic clove, crushed
3 tablespoons rice wine
pinch ground cumin
pinch ground coriander
grated zest of 1 lemon
1 tablespoon chopped dill
freshly ground black pepper

For the watercress:
450g/1lb destalked watercress
1 tablespoon light soy sauce
1 tablespoon rice wine or sherry
1 tablespoon rice vinegar
1 tablespoon sunflower oil

For the garnish:
*30g/1oz cashew nuts, toasted and
    chopped*

1. Mix the marinade ingredients
together in a bowl. Add the pork, mix
well, then cover and refrigerate
overnight.
2. Soak 4 wooden skewers in water for
30 minutes.

3. In a pan of boiling water blanch the
watercress for a few seconds until
wilted, drain and refresh under cold
running water. Squeeze out as much
moisture as possible, then chop and put
into a bowl.
4. Mix together the soy sauce, rice wine,
rice vinegar and oil. Pour over the
watercress and leave to infuse for at
least 30 minutes.
5. Heat the grill.
6. Thread the pork on to the 4 skewers
and baste with the meat marinade.
7. Place under the grill and cook for 3
minutes each side, basting with the
marinade.
8. In a small pan gently reheat the
watercress. Serve with the kebabs
sprinkled with the toasted nuts.

 *LIGHT RED/LOIRE RED*

PORK AND PUMPKIN STRUDEL

SERVES 4

PER PORTION Energy: 1861kj/443kcal
Fat: 18.7g Saturated fat: 3.7g

1 tablespoon olive oil
1 Spanish onion, finely chopped
½ teaspoon ground cinnamon
½ teaspoon ground cumin
½ teaspoon ground coriander
½ teaspoon ground cardamom
1 tablespoon soft brown sugar
450g/1lb pumpkin or butternut squash,
   peeled, deseeded and cut into 2.5cm/1
   inch chunks
450g/1lb lean pork, minced (in the food
   processor)
100ml/3½fl oz medium sherry
150 ml/¼ pint chicken stock (see page
   152)
30g/1oz pecan nuts, toasted and
   chopped
1 tablespoon freshly chopped thyme
8 leaves filo pastry
olive oil to brush
salt and freshly ground black pepper

1. Heat half the oil in a large, non-stick saucepan and cook the onion until soft but not coloured.
2. Add the spices and sugar, turn up the heat and stir until the onion caramelizes.
3. Add the pumpkin or squash to the pan and cook for 2 minutes, stirring continuously and adding a little water if necessary. Transfer to a plate.
4. Set the oven to 190°C/375°F/gas mark 5.
5. Heat the remaining oil in the saucepan and brown the pork until coloured but not dry. Stir with a fork to help break up the pieces.
6. When brown, return the onion and pumpkin mixture to the saucepan with the sherry. Bring to the boil and reduce until syrupy.
7. Pour in the stock, bring to the boil, then cook for 30 minutes or until the pork is tender. Season to taste with salt and pepper. Leave to cool.
8. When cold, add the chopped nuts and thyme.
9. Lay a large sheet of greaseproof paper on a worktop. Place two sheets of filo pastry next to each other on the paper, overlapping them by 5cm/2 inches in the centre. Cover with the remaining sheets of filo pastry, then brush the top layer with olive oil.
10. Spread the cold pork and pumpkin mixture all over the pastry, starting 2cm/1 inch from the top. Roll up fairly tightly, using the greaseproof paper to do so, if it helps.
11. Place the strudel on a baking sheet and brush with olive oil. Bake until golden brown, about 20 minutes.

 RED BURGUNDY/PINOT NOIR

STOCKS AND SAUCES

STOCKS AND SAUCES

Behind every great soup and behind many a sauce, stands a good, strong stock. Stock is flavoured liquid, and the basic flavour can be fish, poultry, meat or vegetable. Stock cubes and bouillon mixes are usually over-salty and they lack the intensely 'real' flavour of properly made stock.

MAKING A STOCK

The secret of stocks is slow, gentle simmering. If the liquid is the slightest bit greasy, vigorous boiling will produce a murky, fatty stock. Skimming, especially for meat stocks, is vital: as fat and scum rise to the surface, they should be lifted off with a slotted spoon, perhaps every 10 or 15 minutes.

Rich, brown stocks are made by first frying or baking the bones, vegetables and scraps of meat until a good, dark, even brown. Only then does the cook proceed with the gentle simmering. Care must be taken not to burn the bones or vegetables: one burned carrot can ruin a gallon of stock. Brown stocks are usually made from red meats or veal, and sometimes only from vegetables for vegetarian dishes.

White stocks are more delicate and are made by simmering only. They are usually based on white poultry or vegetables. The longer meat stocks are simmered, the better flavoured they will be.

Stock can be made in the bottom of an Aga, in which case skimming is unnecessary: the liquid hardly moves, so there is no danger of fat being bubbled into the stock, and it can be lifted off the top when cold.

Fish stocks should never be simmered for more than 30 minutes. After this the bones begin to impart a bitter flavour to the liquid. For a stronger flavour the stock can be strained, skimmed of any scum or fat, then boiled down to reduce and concentrate it.

Similarly, vegetable stocks do not need long cooking. As they contain very little fat, even if the vegetables have been browned in butter before simmering, they are easily skimmed and can then be boiled rapidly to concentrate the flavour. An hour's simmering or half an hour's rapid boiling is generally enough.

The Bones: Most households rarely have anything other than the cooked bones from a roast available for stocks. These will make good stock, but it will be weaker than that made with raw bones. Raw bones are very often free from the butcher, or can be had very cheaply. Get them chopped into manageable small pieces in the shop. A little raw meat, the bloodier the better, gives a rich, very clear liquid.

Water: The water must be cold. If it is hot, the fat in the bones will melt immediately and when the stock begins to boil, much of the fat will be bubbled into the stock. The stock will then be murky, have an unattractive smell and a nasty flavour. Cold water encourages the fat to rise to the surface; it can then be skimmed.

Jellied Stock: Veal bones produce a particularly good stock that will set to a jelly. A pig's trotter added to any stock will have the same jellying effect. Jellied stock will keep longer than liquid stock, but in any event, stocks should be reboiled every 2 or 3 days if kept refrigerated, or every day if kept in a larder, to prevent them going bad.

Salt: Do not add salt to stock. It may be used later for something that is already salty, or boiled down to a concentrated glaze (glace de viande, see page 152), in which case the glaze would be over-salted if the stock contained salt. (Salt does not boil off with the water, but remains in the pan.)

Storage: A good way of storing a large batch of stock is to boil it down to double strength, and to add water only when using. Alternatively, stock can be boiled down to a thick syrupy glaze, which can be used like stock cubes. Many cooks freeze the glaze in ice-cube trays, then turn the frozen cubes into a plastic box in the freezer. They will keep for at least a year if fat-free.

BROWN STOCK

PER 290ml/½ pint Energy: 33.9kj/ 8.1kcal Fat: 0.3g Saturated fat: trace

900g/2lb beef and veal bones
1 tablespoon oil
1 onion, peeled and chopped, skin reserved
1 carrot, roughly chopped
1 celery stalk, chopped
green parts of 2 leeks, chopped (if available)
few mushroom peelings (if available)
parsley stalks
2 bay leaves
6 black peppercorns

1. Heat the oven to 220°C/425°F/gas mark 7.
2. Put the beef and veal bones in a roasting tin and brown in the oven. This may take up to 1 hour. Do not burn.
3. Heat the oil in a large stockpot, add the onion, carrot, celery and leeks and cook until brown, stirring frequently. It is essential that they do not burn.
4. When the bones are well browned, add them to the vegetables with the mushroom peelings, onion skins, parsley stalks, bay leaves and peppercorns. Cover with cold water and bring very slowly to the boil, skimming off any scum as it rises to the surface.
5. When clear of scum, simmer gently for 6–8 hours, or even longer, skimming off the fat as necessary and topping up with water if the level gets very low. The longer it simmers, and the more the liquid reduces by evaporation, the stronger the stock will be.
6. Strain, cool and lift off any remaining fat.

NOTE: Lamb stock can be made using lamb bones, but it is suitable only for lamb dishes.

CHICKEN OR WHITE STOCK

PER 290ml/½ pint Energy: 34kj/8kcal Fat: 0.3g Saturated fat: trace

onion, sliced
celery, sliced
carrot, sliced
chicken or veal bones, skin or flesh
parsley
thyme
bay leaf
black peppercorns

1. Put all the ingredients into a saucepan. Cover generously with water and bring to the boil slowly. Skim off any fat, and/or scum.
2. Simmer for 2–3 hours, skimming frequently and topping up the water level if necessary. The liquid should reduce to half the original quantity.
3. Strain, cool and lift off all the fat.

GLACE DE VIANDE

PER 570ml/1 pint beef stock *(see page 151)*, Absolutely free of fat

1. In a heavy-bottomed saucepan reduce the brown stock by boiling over a steady heat until thick, clear and savoury.
2. Pour into small pots. When cold, cover with polythene or jam covers and secure.
3. Keep in the refrigerator until ready for use.

NOTE: Glace de viande keeps for several weeks and is very useful for enriching sauces.

WHITE FISH STOCK

PER 290ml/½ pint Energy: 34kj/8kcal
Fat: 0.3g Saturated fat: trace

onion, sliced
carrot, sliced
celery, sliced
fish bones, skins, fins, heads or tails
parsley stalks
bay leaf
pinch chopped thyme
black peppercorns

1. Put all the ingredients into a
saucepan, cover with water and bring to
the boil. Reduce the heat to a simmer
and skim off any scum.
2. Simmer for 20 minutes if the fish
bones are small, 30 minutes if large.
Strain.

NOTE: The flavour of fish stock is
impaired if the bones are cooked for too
long. Once strained, however, it may be
strengthened by further boiling and
reducing.

FISH GLAZE

Fish glaze (*glace de poisson*) is simply
very well-reduced, very well-strained
fish stock, which is used to flavour and
enhance fish sauces. It can be kept
refrigerated for about 3 days, or frozen
in ice cube trays and used as required.

VEGETABLE STOCK

PER 290ml/½ pint Energy: 29kj/6.8kcal
Fat: 0.3g Saturated fat: trace

1 onion, roughly chopped
1 leek, roughly chopped
1 large carrot, roughly chopped
2 celery stalks, roughly chopped
few cabbage leaves, roughly shredded
few mushroom stalks
2 garlic cloves, crushed
few parsley stalks
6 black peppercorns
sea salt
1 large bay leaf
6 tablespoons dry white wine
570ml/1 pint water

1. Put all the ingredients in a large saucepan and bring to the boil. Reduce the heat and simmer for 30 minutes, or until the liquid is reduced by half.
2. Strain the stock through a sieve, pressing hard to remove as much liquid as possible. Discard the vegetable pulp. Allow to cool and skim off any fat. Use as required.

COURT BOUILLON

PER 290ml/½ pint Energy: 28kj/6.8kcal
Fat: 0.3g Saturated fat: none

1 litre/1¾ pints water
150ml/¼ pint white wine vinegar
1 carrot, sliced
1 onion, sliced
1 celery stalk
12 black peppercorns
2 bay leaves
2 tablespoons salad oil
salt

1. Bring all the ingredients to the boil in a saucepan, then simmer for 20 minutes.
2. Allow the liquid to cool, then place the fish, meat or vegetables in it and bring slowly to simmering point.

ASPIC

PER 290ml/½ pint Energy: 213kj/ 51kcal Fat: none Saturated fat: none

1 litre/1½ pints well-flavoured,
*   seasoned white stock (see page 152)*
2 egg shells, crushed
2 egg whites
15–30g/ ½–1oz gelatine, as necessary

1. Lift or skim any fat from the stock.
2. Put the stock into a large saucepan and sprinkle on the gelatine. If the stock is liquid when chilled, use 30g/1oz gelatine; if the stock is set when chilled only 15g/½oz will be necessary. Put over a gentle heat to dissolve. Allow to cool.
3. Put the shells and egg whites into the stock. Place over the heat and whisk steadily with a balloon whisk until the mixture begins to boil. Stop whisking immediately and draw the pan off the heat. Allow the mixture to subside. Take care not to break the crust formed by the egg white.
4. Bring the aspic just to the boil again, and again allow to subside. Repeat this once more (the egg white will trap the sediment in the stock and clear the aspic). Allow to cool for 2 minutes.
5. Fix a double layer of fine muslin over a clean basin and carefully strain the aspic through it, taking care to hold the egg-white crust back. When all, or almost all, the liquid is through allow the egg white to slip into the muslin. Strain the aspic again – this time through both egg-white crust and cloth. Do not try to hurry the process by squeezing the cloth, or murky aspic will result.

NOTE: When clearing, it is a good idea to scald the saucepan, sieve and whisk before use.

FRESH TOMATO SAUCE

FULL SAUCE Energy: 923kj/220kcal
Fat: 3.0g Saturated fat: 0.3g

1 large onion, finely chopped
1 tablespoon oil
10 tomatoes, roughly chopped
salt and freshly ground black pepper
pinch sugar
*290ml/ ½ pint chicken stock (see page
    152)*
1 teaspoon fresh thyme leaves

1. Cook the onion in the oil for 3 minutes. Add the tomatoes, salt, pepper and sugar and cook for a further 25 minutes. Add the stock and cook for 5 minutes.
2. Liquidize the sauce and push through a sieve. If it is too thin, reduce, by boiling rapidly, to the desired consistency. Take care: it will spit and has a tendency to catch.
3. Add the thyme. Taste and adjust the seasoning if necessary.

EASY TOMATO SAUCE

FULL SAUCE Energy: 582kj/138kcal
Fat: 0.9g Saturated fat: 0.1g

1 × 400g/14oz tin plum tomatoes
1 small onion, chopped
1 small carrot, chopped
1 celery stalk, chopped
½ garlic clove, crushed
1 bay leaf
parsley stalks
salt and freshly ground black pepper
juice of ½ lemon
dash of Worcestershire sauce (optional)
1 teaspoon sugar
1 teaspoon chopped basil or thyme

1. Put all the ingredients into a heavy-bottomed saucepan, cover and simmer over a medium heat for 30 minutes.
2. Liquidize or process until smooth, then push through a sieve.
3. Return the sauce to the pan. If the sauce is too thin, reduce by boiling rapidly. Check the seasoning, adding more salt or sugar if necessary.

RED PEPPER SAUCE

FULL SAUCE Energy: 932kj/222kcal
Fat: 12.4g Saturated fat: 1.6g

1 onion, finely chopped
1 tablespoon sunflower oil
2 tomatoes, roughly chopped
1 red pepper, peeled (by singeing over a
    flame), deseeded and cut into strips
1 garlic clove, crushed
1 bouquet garni
6 tablespoons water
salt and freshly ground black pepper

1. Cook the onion in the oil until just
beginning to soften. Add the tomatoes,
red pepper, garlic and bouquet garni.
Add the water and season lightly. Cover
and cook slowly for 20 minutes.
2. Liquidize or process until smooth,
then push through a sieve. Chill.

TOMATO AND GINGER SAUCE

SERVES 4

PER PORTION Energy: 151kj/34kcal
Fat: 1.8g Saturated fat: 0.3g

This sauce can be served cold and
uncooked like a salsa, or hot, as
required. If served cold, omit the
ground cumin and coriander, as these
taste unpleasant if not cooked.

450g/1lb tomatoes, peeled, deseeded
    and chopped
1 cm/½ inch fresh ginger, grated
½ red chilli, deseeded and chopped
½ tablespoon olive oil
salt and freshly ground black pepper
½ tablespoon chopped thyme
½ teaspoon ground cumin (for hot
    sauce only)
½ teaspoon ground coriander (for hot
    sauce only)

1. Mix all the ingredients in a bowl. If
to be served cold, chill for 2 hours.
2. To serve hot: dry-fry the spices in a
heavy-bottomed saucepan until
aromatic. Add the remaining
ingredients, bring to the boil and cook
until thick.

TOMATO, BASIL AND OLIVE OIL SAUCE

FULL SAUCE Energy: 989kj/236kcal
Fat: 22.6g Saturated fat: 3.2g

2 tablespoons olive oil
1 garlic clove, flattened but not crushed
2 medium tomatoes, peeled, seeded and finely chopped
4 large basil leaves
salt and freshly ground black pepper

1. Place the oil and garlic in a small saucepan and heat gently for a few minutes to infuse.
2. Remove the garlic and add the tomatoes and basil. Season with salt and pepper. Serve warm.

TOMATO AND MINT SALSA

FULL SAUCE Energy: 712kj/169kcal
Fat: 12.1g Saturated fat: 1.7g

1 shallot, finely diced
1 tablespoon wine vinegar, preferably red
1 tablespoon extra virgin olive oil
4 tomatoes, peeled, deseeded and finely chopped
1 garlic clove, crushed
1 tablespoon chopped mint
salt and freshly ground black pepper

1. Mix together the shallot, vinegar and oil and allow to stand for 10 minutes. Add the tomatoes, garlic and mint and season with salt and pepper.

UNCOOKED PASTA SAUCE

This sauce should be served on the day after it has been made in order to allow the flavours to develop. It can be served with hot or cold pasta.

FULL SAUCE Energy: 1056kj/251kcal
Fat: 13.2g Saturated fat: 1.8g

6 large tomatoes, finely chopped
1 red onion, finely chopped
2 garlic cloves, finely chopped
4 tablespoons chopped fresh basil
1 tablespoon chopped parsley
1 tablespoon extra virgin olive oil
juice of ½ lemon
salt and freshly ground black pepper

1. Put the tomatoes into a sieve and drain them for 30 minutes.
2. Mix the tomatoes with the onion, garlic and herbs. Add the oil and lemon juice. Season to taste with salt and pepper.

SALSA VERDE

PER TABLESPOON Energy: 12kj/3kcal
Fat: trace Saturated fat: trace

½ cucumber, deseeded and diced
½ green chilli, finely diced (see page 91)
1 shallot, finely chopped
grated zest and juice of 1 lime
1 teaspoon caster sugar
1 tablespoon chopped coriander
salt and freshly ground black pepper

1. Mix together all the ingredients and season to taste with salt and pepper. Chill for 2 hours before serving.

BASIL PESTO

This is a reduced-fat version of pesto, but should still be used sparingly.

PER 15g TABLESPOON Energy: 279kj/66kcal Fat: 5.5g Saturated fat: 1.5g

1 garlic clove, peeled
2 large bunches basil leaves
30g/1oz fresh Parmesan cheese, finely grated
5 tablespoons olive oil
salt and freshly ground black pepper

1. Put the garlic and basil in a food processor or liquidizer and whizz to a paste.
2. Add the cheese and the oil. Season to taste with salt and pepper.
3. Keep in a covered jar in the refrigerator for up to 1 week.

NOTE: If the sauce is in danger of curdling, add 1 tablespoon warm water and mix again.

MELLOW PESTO

Pesto is naturally high in fat, so use sparingly.

PER 15g TABLESPOON Energy: 279kj/66kcal Fat: 5.4g Saturated fat: 1.6g

2 tablespoons good-quality olive oil
1 head garlic, cloves unpeeled
generous handful fresh basil
30g/1oz fresh Parmesan cheese, grated (optional)
grated zest of 1 lemon
salt and freshly ground black pepper

1. Break up the head of garlic, but do not peel. Heat the olive oil in a small saucepan and cook the garlic gently for 20 minutes without browning. Remove from the heat and leave to infuse for a further 20 minutes.
2. Strain the olive oil through a fine sieve and reserve. Peel the garlic cloves.
3. In a food processor or liquidizer, process the garlic and basil together to a paste.
4. Add the cheese and the infused oil, then the lemon zest. Season to taste with salt and pepper. Keep in a covered jar in a cool place for up to 1 week.

NOTE: If the sauce is in danger of curdling, add 1 tablespoon warm water and mix again.

PARSLEY PESTO

Pesto is naturally high in fat, so use sparingly.

PER 15g TABLESPOON Energy: 399kj/ 95kcal Fat: 9.2g Saturated fat: 1.6g

1 garlic clove, peeled
1 large handful fresh parsley, roughly chopped
15g/½oz Cheddar cheese, finely grated
2 tablespoons olive oil
salt and freshly ground black pepper

1. Put the garlic and parsley into a food processor liquidizer and whizz to a paste.
2. Quickly mix in the cheese and the oil. Season to taste with salt and pepper.
3. Keep in a covered jar in the refrigerator for up to a week.

NOTE: If the sauce is in danger of curdling, add 1 tablespoon warm water and mix again.

RED PESTO

Pesto is naturally high in fat, so use sparingly.

PER 15g TABLESPOON Energy: 293kj/ 70kcal Fat: 6.6g Saturated fat: 1.3g

55g/2oz dried sun-dried tomatoes
2 garlic cloves, peeled
1 small bunch basil
3 tablespoons good-quality olive oil
30g/1oz pecorino cheese, finely grated
salt and freshly ground black pepper

1. Rinse the tomatoes, then soak in warm water for 20 minutes, or until soft. When ready, drain, dry and chop. Discard the liquid.
2. In a liquidizer or mortar, grind the garlic and basil together to a paste.
3. Whizz in the tomatoes, then add the oil slowly with the motor still running. Whizz in the cheese quickly.
4. Season with salt and pepper.

ROCKET PESTO

Pesto is naturally high in fat, so use sparingly.

PER 15g TABLESPOON Energy: 174kj/ 41kcal Fat: 3.6g Saturated fat: 1.3g

55g/2oz rocket
1 tablespoon olive oil
30g/1oz Parmesan cheese, finely grated
salt and freshly ground black pepper

1. Put all the ingredients into a food processor or liquidizer and process until smooth. Season to taste with salt and pepper. Keep in a covered jar in the refrigerator for up to 1 week.

BASIL AND PARSLEY GREMOLATA

FULL QUANTITY Energy: 661kj/ 157kcal Fat: 1.1g Saturated fat: trace

1 tablespoon chopped basil
2 tablespoons chopped parsley
grated zest of 1 lemon
grated zest of ½ orange
1 garlic clove, crushed
30ml/2 tablespoons dried breadcrumbs

1. Mix all the ingredients together in a bowl. Use within 24 hours – sprinkled over stews, casseroles or other meat dishes.

BLACK BEAN SAUCE

FULL SAUCE Energy: 1186kj/282kcal Fat: 17.3g Saturated fat: 2.3g

3 tablespoons fermented black beans
1 tablespoon sunflower oil
2 spring onions, chopped
1 garlic clove, sliced
2.5cm/1 inch piece fresh ginger, peeled and sliced
2 tablespoons soy sauce.
2 tablespoons sherry
1 teaspoon sugar
290ml/ ½ pint water
2 teaspoons sesame oil

1. Wash the beans again and again.
2. Heat the oil in a saucepan, add the spring onions, garlic and ginger and cook for 1 minute.
3. Add the soy sauce, sherry, beans, sugar and water. Bring slowly to the boil, then simmer for 15 minutes to allow the flavour to infuse.
4. Stir in the sesame oil. Use as required.

NOTE: This sauce is delicious with both chicken and fish.

FRENCH DRESSING

FULL SAUCE Energy: 1249kj/297kcal
Fat: 33g Saturated fat: 4.3g

6 tablespoons olive oil
2 tablespoons wine vinegar
salt and freshly ground black pepper

1. Mix all the ingredients together. Whisk until well emulsified.

VARIATIONS
Oils: olive; sunflower; peanut/arachide; grapeseed.
Walnut; hazelnut; sesame (use 50·50 with plain oil).
Truffle; chilli (use very sparingly, 1 teaspoon to 3 tablespoons plain oil).
Vinegars: white wine; red wine; cider; sherry; champagne; rice wine.
Balsamic.
Flavoured vinegars: tarragon; basil; rosemary; raspberry.
Honeygar (available from healthfood shops).
Citrus juices: lemon; lime; grapefruit.
Mustards: English; Dijon; grainy or any flavoured mustard.
Herbs: tarragon; parsley; basil; chervil; coriander; thyme; chives; dill; mint; fennel fronds.

NOTE: If kept refrigerated, the dressing will form an emulsion more easily when whisked or shaken, and has a slightly thicker consistency. French dressing is naturally high in fat, so use sparingly.

VEGETARIAN MAIN COURSES

VEGETARIAN MAIN COURSES

SPINACH TIMBALES WITH SUN-DRIED TOMATOES AND PINENUTS

SERVES 6

PER PORTION Energy: 601kj/143kcal
Fat: 6.8g Saturated fat: 1.8g

675g/1½lb fresh spinach, cooked,
    drained and roughly chopped
110g/4oz fresh brown or white
    breadcrumbs
2 eggs, lightly beaten
150ml/¼ pint milk
grated nutmeg
grated zest of 1 lemon
1 tablespoon chopped fresh tarragon
salt and freshly ground black pepper
oil

To serve:
1 tablespoon toasted pinenuts
2 tablespoons dried sun-dried tomatoes,
    soaked in hot water for 20 minutes,
    drained and chopped
1 tablespoon chopped fresh basil
4–6 tablespoons Greek yoghurt

1. Process together the spinach, breadcrumbs, eggs, milk, nutmeg, lemon zest, tarragon and salt and pepper. If using a standard-sized processor, it may be necessary to do this in two batches. Taste and adjust the seasoning if necessary.
2. Lightly oil six ramekins; the timbales should turn out quite easily, but to be sure of success the bases can be lined with lightly oiled discs of greaseproof paper.
3. Pile the spinach mixture into the ramekins, cover with tin foil and place in the top half of a steamer. They can be stacked if necessary.
4. Steam for 35–40 minutes.
5. Invert a small plate on top of each ramekin, turn the plate and mould over together and give a sharp, downwards shake. Remove the ramekin.
6. Mix together the pinenuts, sun-dried tomatoes and chopped basil.
7. Put a dollop of fresh yoghurt beside each timbale and garnish with the pinenut mixture.

 *SPICY WHITE*

SPINACH PIE

SERVES 6

PER PORTION Energy: 879kj/210kcal
Fat: 8.3g Saturated fat: 2.6g

*450g/1lb frozen leaf spinach, defrosted,
 drained and finely chopped*
225g/8oz cottage cheese
30g/1oz Parmesan cheese
3 eggs
grated nutmeg
salt and freshly ground black pepper
2 tablespoons olive oil
255g/9oz (9 sheets) filo pastry,

1. Mix together the spinach, cottage
cheese, Parmesan cheese, eggs, nutmeg,
salt and pepper.
2. Preheat the oven to 190°C/375°F/gas
mark 5.
3. Brush a little of the oil on a 28cm/11
inch × 18cm/7 inch baking tray.
4. Brush a sheet of the filo pastry with a
little oil and place on the baking tray: it
should overhang the tin by at least
2.5cm/1 inch. Repeat with 3 more sheets.
5. Cover the pastry with the spinach
mixture, then fold in the overhanging
edges. Place the remaining filo sheets on
top of the pie, oiling between each one
and tucking any excess pastry inside the
dish.
6. Bake for 45 minutes or until the
spinach mixture is firm. Serve hot or
cold.

 *LIGHT RED/MUSCADET DE
SÈVRE ET MAINE*

COURGETTE BRIAM

SERVES 6 as an accompaniment or 4 as a
main meal.

PER MAIN MEAL PORTION Energy:
764kj/182kcal Fat: 3.7g Saturated fat:
0.5g

1 tablespoon sunflower oil
340g/12oz onions, chopped
1 × 400g/14oz tin chopped tomatoes
1 teaspoon tomato purée
1 teaspoon sugar
1 tablespoon chopped parsley
6 tablespoons water
salt and freshly ground black pepper
450g/1lb potatoes, thinly sliced
450g/1lb courgettes, sliced

1. Heat half the oil in a non-stick frying
pan, add the onions and cook gently
over a medium heat until soft and just
browned. Add the tomatoes, tomato
purée, sugar, parsley and 6 tablespoons
water and simmer for 5 minutes. Taste
and season with salt and pepper.
2. Heat the oven to 180°C/350°F/gas
mark 4.
3. Oil a large, ovenproof dish, then
layer the potatoes and courgettes in it.
Season with salt and pepper. Pour over
the tomato sauce, cover and cook for
1½ – 1¾ hours, or until the potatoes are
soft.

 *CABERNET SAUVIGNON*

PASTA AND RISOTTO

PASTA AND RISOTTO

MAKING FRESH PASTA
by C.J. Jackson

The ingredients

Flour: There are many schools of thought on the type of flour that should be used in making fresh pasta. Durum wheat is traditionally used for making dried pasta, with very good reason. Pasta as it dries becomes very brittle and breaks easily; durum wheat flour, being much tougher than other wheat flour, gives dried pasta durability, making it easier to transport.

Fresh egg pasta is usually sold undried and therefore it is not necessary to use durum wheat. Some people, however, favour using plain semolina in the flour to give the dough some durability.

Italian delicatessens sell a strong flour (called 'OO') especially for pasta. The high gluten content makes the dough strong and gives the finished result a perfect texture.

Eggs are used in making fresh pasta. They should be size 2–3 to give the dough enough moisture.

Oil is an important ingredient, giving the dough some elasticity and flavour. Olive oil is the best choice.

Salt and pepper are rarely used in the making of fresh pasta. Salt in particular gives the dough a speckled appearance. It is sufficient to season the water before cooking to give enough flavour.

Water is rarely added in the making of fresh pasta. Again, opinion varies, but water does make the dough tough, so is best avoided. If the dough appears too dry, add extra egg instead.

MAKING THE DOUGH

This can be made by hand or in a pasta machine. Making pasta in a machine is far easier, as the texture of the dough tends to be more consistent. If you enjoy pasta, it is well worth investing in a machine, but we also give instructions for hand-made pasta as follows:

Making pasta dough by hand: Sift the flour on to a clean, scrubbed table top. Make a well in the centre of the flour and drop in the eggs and oil. Using the fingers of one hand, stir the eggs around, gradually incorporating them until a dough begins to form. When most of the flour has been incorporated, begin to knead the dough in the same way as for bread. It should be kneaded until smooth, soft and elastic, which takes about 15 minutes. Avoid using too much flour during the kneading process or the dough will become too dry and will be tough. Enough flour to prevent the pasta from sticking to the table is sufficient.

Once the dough is kneaded, wrap it well in cling film and leave to relax at room temperature for 30 minutes. If you plan to leave the dough longer, it should be refrigerated. Carefully wrapped, the dough can be frozen at this stage.

Making pasta dough in a food processor: Put all the ingredients into the food processor; there is no need to sift the flour as the cutting action of the blade will aerate it. Process only until the mixture resembles very fine breadcrumbs: if the dough is allowed to come together in the machine, it will be too wet. Work the mixture into a dough by hand. No hand-kneading is required as the machine will have done all that is necessary. Wrap and leave to relax as described above.

Rolling pasta dough by hand: If the pasta dough has been in the refrigerator, allow it to come to room temperature for 20–30 minutes before rolling. A very cold dough is difficult to roll.

Lightly flour a clean work surface and roll the dough out as thinly as possible: ideally you should be able to read a newspaper through it. Cut into the shape required. Long noodles should be allowed to dry partially by hanging them over a clean chair back for at least 30 minutes. Shorter ones should be dried on a wire rack or clean tea towel. If not dried in this way, the pasta will stick together when cooked or stored.

Rolling pasta dough through a pasta machine: Bring the dough to room temperature (see above). Lightly flour the dough and roll first through the widest setting of the rollers; this also kneads the dough a little. Give the dough 2–3 more rollings at thinner settings to make it as thin as possible.

Cut as required and allow to dry as described above.

COMMONEST NOODLE SHAPES

Cannelloni: Rectangles about the size of a side plate. They are rolled and generally stuffed (like a pancake) after boiling, then reheated.

Tagliatelle (fettucine): Thin ribbons of pasta, usually served with a sauce.

Lasagne: Wide strips usually used in alternate layers with a savoury mixture.

Ravioli: Flat sheets used to form small stuffed envelopes, which are then boiled and served with or without sauce.

Spaghetti: Originally made by pulling the dough into thin strands, now usually made by machine.

Macaroni: Made commercially into short tube-like pieces.

COOKING PASTA

Whether using home-made or bought fresh pasta, or dried pasta, cook in a large saucepan of fast-boiling water to which 1 teaspoon salt and 1 tablespoon oil has been added to prevent the pasta from sticking together. Choose a saucepan large enough to allow for expansion of the pasta during cooking. Cook the pasta until *al dente* (literally 'to the bite') or *just* tender. Obviously, dried pasta will take longer to cook than fresh. Drain lightly in a colander. Overdraining will make the pasta dry and it will stick together.

EGG PASTA

SERVES 6

PER PORTION Energy: 1349kj/321kcal
Fat: 6.5g Saturated fat: 1.4g.

450g/1lb strong 'OO' flour
pinch salt
4 eggs
1 tablespoon oil

1. Sift the flour and salt on to a wooden board. Make a well in the centre and drop in the eggs and oil.
2. Using the fingers of one hand, mix together the eggs and oil and gradually draw in the flour. The mixture should be a very stiff dough.
3. Knead until smooth and elastic (about 15 minutes). Wrap in cling film and leave to relax in a cool place for 30 minutes.
4. Roll out one small piece of dough at a time until paper-thin. Cut into shapes of the required size.
5. Allow to dry (unless making lasagne or ravioli), hanging over a clean chair back if long noodles, lying on a wire rack or clean dry tea towel if small ones, for at least 30 minutes before boiling.

VARIATIONS

Tomato pasta: Add approximately 2 teaspoons tomato purée.
Herb pasta: Add plenty of chopped very fresh herbs to taste, such as parsley, thyme and tarragon.
Beetroot pasta: Add 1 small cooked, puréed beetroot.
NOTE: If more or less pasta is required, the recipe can be altered on a pro-rata basis: for example, a 340g/12oz quantity of flour calls for a pinch of salt, 3 eggs and 1 scant tablespoon oil.

SPINACH PASTA

SERVES 4

PER PORTION Energy: 1417kj/337kcal
Fat: 4.3g Saturated fat: 1.0g

225g/8oz spinach, cooked
340g/12oz strong 'OO' flour
pinch of salt
2 eggs

1. Chop or liquidize the spinach and push through a sieve to get a fairly dry paste.
2. Sift the flour and salt on to a wooden board. Make a well in the centre and drop in the eggs and spinach. Using the fingers of one hand, mix together the eggs and spinach, gradually drawing in the flour. The mixture should be a stiff dough.
3. Knead until smooth and elastic, about 15 minutes. Wrap in cling film and leave to relax in a cool place for 30 minutes.
4. Roll out one small piece of dough at a time until paper-thin. Cut into the required shape and size. Allow to dry (hanging over a clean chair back if long noodles, or lying on a wire rack or clean tea towel if small) for at least 30 minutes before cooking.

SAFFRON NOODLES

SERVES 6

PER PORTION Energy: 837kj/199kcal
Fat: 6.9g Saturated fat: 1.6g

285g/10oz strong 'OO' flour
salt and freshly ground white pepper
2 whole eggs
3 egg yolks
1 tablespoon olive oil
½ teaspoon saffron strands soaked in 2
  tablespoons boiling water

1. Put all the ingredients into a food processor and process until the mixture forms a dough. Alternatively sift the flour into a bowl, add the salt and pepper, make a well in the centre and add the eggs, oil and saffron liquid. Gradually mix the flour into the liquid using your hand. Eventually draw it together into a ball of dough and knead until elastic. Wrap and leave to relax.
2. Roll out the pasta as thinly as possible. Dust with flour and roll up like a Swiss roll. Cut as thinly as possible. Unravel the pasta, dust with flour and place on a tray to dry slightly.

PASTA WITH MUSHROOMS AND GINGER SAUCE

This recipe calls for Japanese soy sauce; if it is not available, light soy sauce is the best substitute. If you cannot obtain mirin (Japanese rice wine), light muscovado sugar or a sweet sherry can be used instead.

SERVES 4

PER PORTION Energy: 3218kj/766kcal
Fat: 10.5g Saturated fat: 3.6g

1 tablespoon sesame seed oil
2 shallots, sliced
285g/10oz field mushrooms, sliced
285g/10oz shiitake mushrooms, sliced
285g/10oz oyster mushrooms sliced
150ml/¼ pint mirin
5 tablespoons soy sauce
2.5cm/1 inch fresh ginger, grated
2 pieces preserved ginger, finely
  chopped
salt and freshly ground black pepper
450g/1lb tagliatelle
2 tablespoons freshly chopped chives
55g/2oz Parmesan cheese, finely grated

1. Heat the oil in a large, heavy-bottomed saucepan and sweat the shallots until soft but not coloured.
2. Add the mushrooms and cook until soft, 6 minutes. Add the mirin and soy sauce, bring to the boil and simmer gently until the liquid has reduced by half. Add both the gingers. Season to taste.
3. In a large pan of boiling salted water cook the tagliatelle until *al dente*. Drain and toss with the mushroom sauce. Transfer to a large dish, sprinkle with the chives and Parmesan and serve immediately.

 *PINOT BLANC/RIESLING*

BLACK AND WHITE PASTA WITH PRAWNS

SERVES 4

PER PORTION Energy: 2285kj/544kcal
Fat: 7.9g Saturated fat: 1.1g

*450g/1lb raw prawns heads removed, in
  their shells*
½ tablespoon chilli oil
3 tablespoons vodka
1 tablespoon sunflower oil
2 shallots, finely chopped
zest of 1 lime
1 teaspoon horseradish relish
salt and freshly ground black pepper
225g/8oz white tagliatelle
225g/8oz black tagliatelle
2 tablespoons freshly chopped dill

1. Peel and devein the prawns (see page
89). Wash and pat dry. Put into a bowl,
pour in the chilli oil and vodka and mix
gently. Cover and refrigerate for 1 hour.
2. Heat the sunflower oil in a wok and
add the shallots.
3. Lift the prawns from the marinade
with a perforated spoon, add to the wok
in a single layer and fry for about 1
minute. Reduce the heat if they begin to
burn. Turn over to fry on the other side
for about 1 minute. Transfer to a plate.
Pour the marinade into the pan and add
the lime zest and horseradish relish.
Reduce the liquid by boiling until
syrupy. Return the prawns to the pan
and season to taste with salt and
pepper.

4. In a large pan of boiling salted water
cook the tagliatelle until *al dente*, about
3 minutes. Drain and toss with the
prawn mixture. Stir in half the chopped
dill.
5. Transfer to a large dish, sprinkle with
the remaining dill and serve.

 *SPICY WHITE*

SPAGHETTI WITH MUSSELS

Many people concerned about their heart avoid mussels because they are quite high in cholesterol. However, it is more important to cut down on saturated fat in our diet than to worry about occasionally eating high-cholesterol foods.

SERVES 4

PER PORTION Energy: 2611kj/624kcal Fat: 11.5g Saturated fat: 1.7g

1.3kg/3lb mussels in their shells
285g/10oz spaghetti
150ml/¼ pint dry white wine
1 tablespoon olive oil
3 garlic cloves, crushed
230g/7½oz tin chopped tomatoes
4 tablespoons chopped parsley
salt and freshly ground black pepper

1. Scrub the mussels, remove any barnacles with a sharp knife, pull off their beards and wash in several changes of water. Discard any mussels that are broken, those that do not close when they are tapped and any that feel light for their size.
2. In a large saucepan of boiling salted water cook the spaghetti until *al dente*, about 10–12 minutes. Drain and keep warm.
3. Place the mussels in a large saucepan with the wine, cover with a lid and cook for 3–5 minutes, or until the mussels have opened.

4. Remove the mussels from the pan with a perforated spoon and place in a colander. Cover with a lid or tea towel to keep warm. Throw away any mussels that have not opened.
5. Reduce the cooking liquid by half by boiling rapidly.
6. Heat the oil in a non-stick frying pan, add the garlic and cook for 2 minutes. Add the tomatoes and cook for 5 minutes. Add the reduced cooking liquor, parsley, salt and pepper.
7. Remove the mussels from their shells. Reserve a few for garnish, and add the rest to the tomato sauce.
8. Heat together the sauce and drained spaghetti in a large saucepan. Serve in large bowls garnished with the reserved mussels.

 *PINOT GRIGIO/ROSÉ*

ASPARAGUS RISOTTO

SERVES 4

PER PORTION Energy: 1829kj/437kcal
Fat: 8.1g Saturated fat: 2.1g

450g/1lb asparagus
1.2 litres/2 pints chicken stock (see page
*   152) or vegetable water*
1 yellow pepper, quartered and
*   deseeded*
1 tablespoon olive oil
1 Spanish onion, finely chopped
310g/11oz risotto rice
150ml/¼ pint dry vermouth
1 tablespoon freshly chopped basil
15g/½oz pistachio nuts
30g/1oz Parmesan cheese, grated
salt and freshly ground black pepper

To serve:
extra Parmesan

1. Heat the grill to its highest setting.
2. In a pan of boiling salted water cook
the asparagus for about 6 minutes or
until tender. Strain and refresh under
cold water until cool. Cut the tips off on
the diagonal and reserve.
3. Gently heat the stock or vegetable
water.
4. Put the asparagus stems into a food
processor and process until smooth. Set
aside.
5. Grill the pepper, skin side uppermost,
until the skin is black and blistered. Put
in a plastic bag, seal and leave to cool.
6. Heat the oil in a large, heavy-

bottomed saucepan and gently cook the
onion until soft but not coloured. Add
the rice and cook, stirring, for 1 minute.
Add the vermouth, bring to the boil and
cook until the wine is absorbed. Stir
gently all the time.
7. Gradually add the warmed stock to
the rice, stirring continuously until all
the stock has been absorbed; this may
take up to 25 minutes.
8. Add the asparagus purée. When the
peppers are cool, remove from the bag,
peel off the blackened skin and slice the
flesh. Add to the risotto with the
asparagus tips, basil and pistachio nuts.
9. Remove the pan from the heat and
stir in the cheese. Season to taste with
salt and plenty of pepper. Serve
immediately with the extra cheese
handed separately.

 CHARDONNAY/PINOT GRIS

RADICCHIO RISOTTO

SERVES 4

PER PORTION Energy: 2272kj/542kcal
Fat: 9.5g Saturated fat: 2.7g

1 red pepper, quartered and deseeded
1 tablespoon good-quality olive oil
2 red onions, chopped
1 garlic clove, crushed
1 tablespoon freshly chopped rosemary
310g/11oz risotto rice
150ml/¼ pint red vermouth or red wine
860ml/1½ pints chicken stock (see page
*   152) or vegetable water*
450g/1lb radicchio, shredded
8 dried sun-dried tomatoes, soaked in
*   hot water for 20 minutes, drained and*
*   shredded*
3 anchovies, rinsed very well and sliced
*   (optional)*
1 tablespoon pumpkin seeds, toasted
*   (optional)*
30g/1oz fresh Parmesan cheese, grated
salt and freshly ground black pepper

1. Heat the grill to its highest setting.
2. Grill the pepper, skin side uppermost, until the skin is black and blistered. Put into a plastic bag, seal and leave to cool.
3. Heat the oil and cook the onion until soft but not coloured. Add the rice and cook, stirring, for 1 minute. Pour in the vermouth or wine, bring to the boil and cook until the wine is absorbed, about 2 minutes. Stir gently all the time.
4. In a second pan heat the chicken stock or vegetable water, and gradually add it to the rice, stirring continuously and gently until all the stock has been absorbed. This can take up to 20 minutes.
5. When the peppers are cool, remove from the bag, peel off the blackened skin and slice the flesh.
6. Add the peppers, radicchio, tomatoes, anchovies (if using) and pumpkin seeds to the pan. Heat through.
7. Remove the pan from the heat and stir in half the cheese. Season to taste and serve straight away with the remaining cheese handed separately.

 *LIGHT RED*

MUSHROOM RISOTTO

Risottos are usually made with a great deal of fat but this recipe shows that it is possible 'to have your cake and eat it'.

SERVES 4

PER PORTION Energy: 1632kj/390kcal
Fat: 7.4g Saturated fat: 0.7g

1 tablespoon olive oil
1 onion, finely chopped
225g/8oz oyster mushrooms, sliced
225g/8oz shiitake mushrooms, sliced
1 garlic clove, crushed
¼ teaspoon chilli powder
310g/11oz risotto rice
100ml/3½fl oz dry white wine
1.2 litres/2 pints hot vegetable stock (see
*   page 154)*
salt and freshly ground black pepper
3 tablespoons chopped fresh parsley

1. Heat the oil in a large saucepan and cook the onion over a medium heat for 5–10 minutes. Add the mushrooms, garlic and chilli powder and cook for a further 2 minutes. Add the rice and stir for 2 minutes. Add the wine and simmer, uncovered, stirring frequently, until all the wine has been absorbed, about 3 minutes.
2. Stir in 100ml/3½fl oz hot stock, stirring until absorbed. Continue until all the stock is used and the rice is cooked. The whole process should take about 20–25 minutes. Season to taste with salt and pepper.
3. Stir in the parsley and serve.

 *RHÔNE RED/SHIRAZ*

PIZZAS

PIZZAS

PIZZA DOUGH

PER PORTION Energy: 1744kj/415kcal
Fat: 4.2g Saturated fat: 0.6g

Makes 4 × 25cm/10 inch pizzas
30g/1oz fresh yeast
pinch of sugar
290ml/½ pint lukewarm water
450g/1lb plain flour
1 teaspoon salt
1 tablespoon olive oil

1. Cream the yeast with the sugar and 2
tablespoons of the water.
2. Sift the flour with the salt and make a
well in the centre. Pour in the yeast
mixture, the remaining water and the
oil. Mix together until it turns into a
soft but not wet dough. Add more
water or flour if necessary.
3. Turn out on to a floured surface and
knead well for about 10 minutes, until
the dough is smooth. Place in a clean,
oiled bowl and cover with greased
polythene. Leave in a warm place until
the dough has doubled in bulk. Use as
required.

RED PIZZA

SERVES 4

PER PORTION Energy: 2373kj/565kcal
Fat: 12.4g Saturated fat: 1.8g

1 tablespoon olive oil
3 medium red onions, finely sliced
2 red peppers
1 head radicchio
1 red chilli, finely chopped (see page 91)
1 teaspoon tomato purée
1 garlic clove, crushed
1 tablespoon chopped fresh oregano
1 quantity pizza dough (see page 183)
8 dried sun-dried tomatoes, soaked in
    hot water for 20 minutes
4 anchovies, chopped
2 tablespoons red pesto (see page 161)
2 tablespoons balsamic vinegar
salt and freshly ground black pepper .

For the garnish:
fresh oregano sprigs
Parmesan shavings, optional

1. Heat the oil in a large saucepan and
sweat the onions until soft but not
coloured.
2. Heat the grill to its highest setting.
Cut the peppers into quarters removing
the stalk, inner membrane and seeds.
3. Grill the peppers, skin side
uppermost, until the skin is black and
blistered. Put into a plastic bag, seal and
leave to cool.
4. Remove and discard the outer leaves
of radicchio and cut the head into eight,
retaining the core.

5. Set the oven to 200°C/400°F/gas
mark 6.
6. When the onions are tender, add the
chilli, tomato purée, garlic and oregano.
Cook for 1 minute, stirring. Add the
radicchio and cook until soft, stirring
carefully to avoid breaking the
radicchio pieces.
7. When the peppers are cool, remove
the blackened skin and slice the flesh.
8. Divide the pizza dough into four and
place on four floured baking sheets.
Using the heel of your hand, push and
punch the dough into 25cm/10 inch
circles.
9. Spread the pizza bases with the red
onion and radicchio mixture, leaving a
2.5cm/1 inch margin all around. Drain,
dry and slice the soaked tomatoes, then
divide equally between the pizzas with
the anchovies and red peppers. Spread
with the red pesto, sprinkle with the
vinegar and season lightly. The pizzas
can sit for up to 1 hour before they are
baked.
10. Bake for 15–20 minutes. Garnish
with fresh oregano and shavings of
Parmesan, if desired.

 *LIGHT ITALIAN RED*

Radicchio Risotto

Baked New Potatoes en Papilotte

Baked Golden Vegetables

Baked Exotic Fruits

Strawberry and Rosemary Sorbet; Apricot and Elderflower Sorbet;
Strawberry, Raspberry and Cardamom Granita

Rhubarb and Orange Terrine

Citrus and Cranberry Fruit Salad

White Bread; Ballymaloe Brown Bread; Hazelnut and Raisin Rolls;
Brown Soda Bread; Garlic Bread; Grissini; Italian Bread

YELLOW PIZZA

SERVES 4

PER PORTION Energy: 2606kj/620kcal
Fat: 15.8g Saturated fat: 3.3g

1 tablespoon olive oil
1 Spanish onion, finely chopped
2 yellow peppers
2 orange peppers
225g/8oz yellow courgettes or baby
  yellow squash
2 garlic cloves, crushed
1 tablespoon chopped fresh thyme
5 tablespoons dry white vermouth
1 quantity pizza dough (see page 183)
110g/4oz yellow cherry tomatoes,
  halved
55g/2oz feta cheese
30g/1oz pinenuts
salt and freshly ground black pepper

1. Heat the oil in a saucepan and cook the onions until soft but not coloured.
2. Heat the grill to its highest setting. Cut the peppers into quarters, removing the stalk, inner membrane and seeds.
3. Grill the peppers, skin side uppermost, until the skin is black and blistered. Put into a plastic bag, seal and leave to cool.
4. Using a vegetable peeler, slice the courgettes into ribbons. If using yellow squash, slice very finely.
5. When the onions are tender, add the garlic, thyme and vermouth, cooking until the juices are syrupy. Taste and season with salt and pepper.

6. Set the oven to 200°C/400°F/gas mark 6.
7. When the peppers are cool, remove from the bag, peel off the blackened skin and slice the flesh.
8. Divide the pizza dough into four and place on four floured baking sheets. Using the heel of your hand, push and punch the dough into 25cm/10 inch circles.
9. Spread the pizza bases with the onion mixture, then sprinkle with the courgettes, leaving a 2.5cm/1 inch margin all around. Divide the peppers, tomatoes (cut side up), feta and pinenuts between the pizzas. They can sit for up to 1 hour before they are baked.
10. Bake for 15–20 minutes.

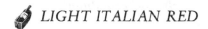 *LIGHT ITALIAN RED*

GREEN PIZZA

SERVES 4

PER PORTION Energy: 2504kj/596kcal
Fat: 14.7g Saturated fat: 3.8g

1 tablespoon olive oil
2 Spanish onions, finely sliced
1 garlic clove, crushed
5 tablespoons dry white vermouth
   (optional)
225g/8oz courgettes
1 quantity pizza dough (see page 183)
450g/1lb spinach, blanched, refreshed,
   chopped and squeezed dry
30g/1oz green olives, stoned
2 tablespoons basil pesto (see page 160)
55g/2oz fresh rocket leaves
55g/2oz goat's cheese, crumbled

1. Heat the olive oil in a saucepan and
sweat the onions until soft but not
coloured. When tender, add the garlic
and vermouth, if using; cook until soft
and the juices are syrupy.
2. Using a vegetable peeler, slice the
courgettes into fine ribbons.
3. Set the oven to 200°C/400°F/gas
mark 6.
4. Divide the dough into four and place
on four floured baking sheets. Using the
heel of your hand, push and punch the
dough into 25cm/10 inch circles.
5. Spread the pizza bases with the onion
mixture, leaving a 2.5cm/1 inch margin
all round. Spread the cooked spinach
over the onion mixture.
6. Divide the courgettes, olives and

pesto between the pizzas. They can sit
for up to 1 hour before they are baked.
7. Bake for 15 minutes, then sprinkle
with the rocket leaves and crumbled
goat's cheese. Return to the oven and
bake for 5 more minutes.

 *LIGHT ITALIAN RED*

VEGETABLE AND SIDE DISHES

VEGETABLE AND SIDE DISHES

RAITA

PER 15ml TABLESPOON Energy:
24kj/5.7kcal Fat: 0.1g Saturated fat:
0.1g

¼ cucumber
150ml/¼ pint natural yoghurt
1 tablespoon finely chopped mint
salt and freshly ground black pepper

1. Chop the cucumber into very fine
dice and pat dry with absorbent paper
to remove any excess moisture. Mix all
the ingredients together and season with
salt and pepper.

Note: There are very many recipes for
raita, some of which include garlic or
paprika. This is a simple version which
can be adapted.

CHINESE FRIED RICE

This is an adaptation of Yan-kit So's recipe for mixed fried rice from *The Wok Cook Book* by Yan-kit So (Piatkus Publishing, London, 1985). As she says, this recipe can be changed to use up leftovers, in the refrigerator as long as you keep the essential ingredients – rice, spring onions and egg.

SERVES 4–6

PER PORTION Energy: 2133kj/508kcal
Fat: 9.8g saturated fat: 2.2g

1 tablespoon sunflower oil
1 × 100g/4oz tin bamboo shoots, drained
½ cucumber, diced
110g/4oz petit pois, cooked
6 spring onions, chopped, white and green parts separated
2 eggs, lightly beaten with ¼ teaspoon salt
Steamed rice (see page 191)
½ teaspoon salt
225g/8oz cooked chicken, diced
1 tablespoon light soy sauce or to taste

1. Heat the wok, add half the oil and, when hot, stir-fry the bamboo shoots and cucumber. Remove and mix with the petit pois. Wipe the wok clean.
2. Heat the remaining oil, add the white spring onions and stir-fry for 30 seconds. Add the egg and let it set very slightly. Add the rice and stir-fry vigorously to combine thoroughly. When hot, add the salt and chicken.
3. Return the bamboo shoots, cucumber and peas to the wok and stir until very hot. Add the soy sauce and green spring onions. Stir and add extra soy sauce to taste.

STEAMED RICE

This recipe has been taken from *The Wok Cook Book* by Yan-kit So (Piatkus Publishing, London, 1985).

SERVES 6

PER PORTION Energy: 1017kj/242kcal Fat: 2.5g Saturated fat: 0.2g

370g/13oz long-grain white rice
450ml/16fl oz water
1 tablespoon vegetable oil

1. Wash the rice in several changes of water until the water no longer appears milky. Drain well.
2. Put the rice in either a cake tin or ovenproof glass pie dish. Add the water and oil. Put the tin or dish on a steaming stand in the wok.
3. Steam, covered, over a high heat for about 25 minutes if using a cake tin or 35 minutes if using a glass dish. The rice should be firm but cooked through. Fluff up and serve.

BOILED BROWN RICE

Brown rices vary enormously, and although this method is suitable for the majority of them, some may require longer, slower cooking.

PER PORTION Energy: 825kj/196kcal Fat: 1.5g Saturated fat: 0.4g

55g/2oz brown rice per person
salt

1. Cook the rice in a large amount of boiling salted water for 20 minutes. Drain well.

PERSIAN RICE

SERVES 4

PER PORTION Energy: 845kj/202kcal
Fat: 0.3g Saturated fat: trace

285g/10oz basmati rice, well rinsed
3 tablespoons chopped fresh parsley
3 tablespoons chopped fresh coriander
1 tablespoon chopped fresh mint
salt and freshly ground black pepper

1. Bring a large pan of water to the boil and add the rice. Simmer for 8 minutes and drain well.
2. Return the rice to the saucepan, add the herbs, salt and pepper and cover with a lid. Leave undisturbed for 5 minutes.
3. Remove the lid, fluff up the rice and serve.

TABBOULEH

SERVES 4

PER PORTION Energy: 686kj/164kcal
Fat: 4.3g Saturated fat: 0.5g

170g/6oz bulgar wheat
2 tablespoons lemon juice
1 tablespoon olive oil
salt and freshly ground black pepper
4 tomatoes, diced
1 small onion, finely chopped
30g/1oz chopped fresh parsley
1 tablespoon chopped fresh mint

1. Soak the bulgar wheat in plenty of cold water for 20 minutes, or until soft and swollen. Rinse and drain, squeezing out any excess water. Spread the wheat out on absorbent paper or a tea towel and dry thoroughly.
2. Place the bulgar with the lemon juice, oil, salt and pepper in a bowl for about 30 minutes, or until it has absorbed the dressing.
3. Add the tomatoes, onion, parsley and mint.

WARM TABBOULEH WITH YELLOW PEPPERS

SERVES 4

PER PORTION Energy: 1120kj/267kcal
Fat: 4.6g Saturated fat: 0.6g

170g/6oz bulgar cracked wheat
1 tablespoon olive oil
1 onion, chopped
2 yellow peppers, deseeded, skinned and
  diced
6 dried sun-dried tomatoes, soaked in
  hot water for 20 minutes, drained and
  chopped
1 tablespoon chopped basil
1 tablespoon balsamic vinegar
salt and freshly ground black pepper

1. Soak the bulgar in warm water for 1
hour – it will expand greatly.
2. Heat the oil in a saucepan, add the
onion and cook until soft but not
coloured.
3. Drain the bulgar wrap in a clean tea
towel and squeeze out the moisture.
Spread the bulgar on a tray lined with
absorbent paper to dry further: it
should be moist, neither wet nor dry.
4. Transfer to the saucepan with the
onions, add the yellow pepper and
tomatoes, stir and heat through.
5. When ready to serve, stir in the basil
and vinegar. Season to taste with salt
and pepper.

BAKED NEW POTATOES EN PAPILLOTE

We love these scented potatoes with
their slightly crinkly skin. They must be
baked in silicone paper rather than tin
foil so that they do not steam. They
take a surprisingly long time to cook.

SERVES 4

PER PORTION Energy: 607kj/145kcal
Fat: 3.3g Saturated fat: 0.4g

675g/1½lb new potatoes, washed and
  dried
1 tablespoon sunflower oil
salt and freshly ground black pepper
1 sprig fresh rosemary
4 garlic cloves, unpeeled

1. Preheat the oven to 200°C/400°F/gas
mark 6.
2. Place the potatoes on a large piece of
silicone paper. Turn them lightly in the
oil and season with salt and pepper.
3. Add the rosemary and garlic and
wrap the potatoes up in the silicone
paper in such a way that the steam does
not escape.
4. Bake for about 1 hour, or until
tender.

BRAISED SWEET POTATOES WITH PEPPERS AND LIME

SERVES 6

PER PORTION Energy: 447kj/106kcal Fat: 2.3g Saturated fat: 0.4g

170g/6oz onion, finely sliced
1 tablespoon, olive oil
170g/6oz yellow pepper, deseeded,
   quartered and finely sliced
4oz/110g red pepper, deseeded,
   quartered and finely sliced
salt and freshly ground black pepper
grated zest of 1 lime
450g/1lb sweet potatoes (peeled weight)
190–250ml/6–8fl oz vegetable stock (see
   page 154)
juice of 1 lime

For the garnish:
lime leaves or continental parsley, finely
   chopped

1. Set the oven to 170°C/325°F gas mark 3.
2. Sweat onion in the olive oil in a covered frying pan over a gentle heat until soft but not coloured.
3. Add the peppers and cook, covered, until tender. Season with salt and plenty of black pepper and stir in the lime zest.
4. Slice the sweet potatoes thickly and layer with the cooked vegetables in a lidded casserole, starting and finishing with a vegetable layer. Season each layer. Pour in enough stock to come halfway up the dish, cover and cook for 40 minutes, or until tender.
5. Purée 1 heaped tablespoon cooked sweet potato with 2–3 tablespoons cooking liquid. Return to the casserole and stir in to thicken the liquid.
6. Add enough lime juice to sharpen the sauce. Scatter the dish with chopped lime leaves or parsley, and serve.

ROOT VEGETABLE BOULANGÈRE

SERVES 4

PER PORTION Energy: 784kj/187kcal
Fat: 5.4g Saturated fat: 1.0g

1 tablespoon olive oil
1 small onion, chopped
extra oil for greasing
225g/8oz potatoes, thinly sliced
225g/8oz sweet potatoes, thinly sliced
225g/8oz parsnips, sliced
225g/8oz celeriac, sliced
290ml/ ½ pint chicken stock (see page 152)
salt and freshly ground black pepper
nutmeg
1 tablespoon grated Parmesan cheese

1. Heat the oven to 190°C/325°F/gas mark 5.
2. Heat the oil in a small saucepan and cook the onion until soft but not coloured.
3. Lightly oil a pie dish. Arrange the root vegetables in alternate layers with the onion, arranging the top layer in overlapping slices of each vegetable to create distinct stripes.
4. Season the stock with salt, pepper and grated nutmeg, and pour into the pie dish. Press the vegetables down firmly – they should be completely submerged in the stock.
5. Cover and bake in the oven for about 50 minutes. Uncover, scatter with the Parmesan and bake for a further 50 minutes or until the vegetables are tender when pierced with a table knife and the top browned. (If the vegetables are tender but not brown, pour off any excess liquid and return the dish to the oven or brown under a hot grill.)

MASHED POTATOES

SERVES 4

PER PORTION Energy: 590kj/139kcal
Fat: 0.8g Saturated fat: 0.4g

675g/1 ½lb potatoes, peeled
about 150ml/ ¼ pint skimmed milk
salt and pepper
a little grated nutmeg

1. Boil the potatoes in salted water until tender. Drain thoroughly.
2. Push the potatoes through a sieve or mouli. Return them to the dry saucepan. Heat carefully, stirring to allow the potato to steam dry.
3. Push the mass of potato to one side of the pan. Put the exposed part of the pan over direct heat and pour in the milk. Tilt the pan to allow the milk to boil without burning the potato.
4. When the milk is boiling, or near it, beat it into the potato. Seasonb with salt, pepper and nutmeg.

STIR-FRIED VEGETABLES

This recipe can be adapted according to what you have in your refrigerator, but mangetout and baby sweetcorn are usually included.

SERVES 4

PER PORTION Energy: 346kj/82kcal
Fat: 4.1g Saturated fat: 0.5g

1 tablespoon sunflower oil
*2.5cm/1 inch piece fresh ginger, peeled
    and cut into slivers*
1 garlic clove, peeled and cut into slivers
*110g/4oz baby corn, cut in half
    lengthways*
110g/4oz mangetout, topped
3 celery stalks, cut into julienne strips
*2 carrots, peeled and cut into julienne
    strips*
*1 red pepper, peeled (by singeing over a
    flame), deseeded and cut into strips*
3 spring onions, sliced diagonally
85g/3oz Chinese leaves, finely shredded
2 tablespoons soy sauce
1 teaspoon sesame oil

1. Heat the oil in a wok. Add the ginger and garlic and fry gently for a moment or two.
2. Add the baby corn, mangetout, celery and carrots. Stir-fry for 1–2 minutes.
3. Add the red pepper, spring onions and Chinese leaves. Stir-fry until the leaves begin to wilt. Add the soy sauce and sesame oil and serve immediately.

BAKED GOLDEN VEGETABLES

SERVES 4

PER PORTION Energy: 645kj/154kcal
Fat: 8.1g Saturated fat: 1.9g

2 yellow peppers
2 red peppers
4 shallots, peeled
4 garlic cloves, unpeeled
2 tablespoons wholegrain French
  mustard
225g/8oz cherry tomatoes, yellow if
  possible
1 tablespoon good-quality olive oil
1 tablespoon chopped fresh oregano
salt and freshly ground black pepper
30g/1oz Parmesan cheese, grated

1. Set the oven to 200°C/400°F/gas mark 6.
2. Place the peppers and shallots in a roasting tin and heat in the oven for 20 minutes.
3. Add the garlic to the roasting tin and bake for a further 20 minutes.
4. Remove from the oven and reduce the heat to 180°C/350°F/gas mark 4.
5. When cool enough to handle, remove the stems from the peppers, then peel and deseed, reserving any juices.
6. Peel the garlic, then mash and mix it with the mustard.
7. Place the peppers, shallots and tomatoes in a greased ovenproof dish and spread with the garlic and mustard mixture. Drizzle with the olive oil, sprinkle with oregano and season with salt and pepper.
8. Place in the oven and bake for 15 minutes. Sprinkle with the Parmesan before serving.

DRY CAULIFLOWER CURRY

This curry is an accompaniment to serve with pilau rice, a meat or vegetarian curry such as beef dhansak, or curried black-eye beans and raita.

SERVES 4

PER PORTION Energy: 545kj/130kcal Fat: 5.9g Saturated fat: 0.4g

4 teaspoons vegetable oil
1 teaspoon cumin seeds
5cm/2 inches fresh ginger, peeled and finely chopped
½ teaspoon hot chilli seasoning
1 tablespoon ground coriander
2 teaspoons turmeric
6 tablespoons water
salt and freshly ground black pepper
2 small or 1 large cauliflower, chopped into very small florets
2 teaspoons garam masala
2 teaspoons lemon juice

1. Heat the oil in a large frying pan or wok. Add the cumin seeds and when they begin to sizzle, add the ginger. Stir and cook for a few minutes until it begins to brown. Add the chilli, coriander and turmeric. Add 6 tablespoons water and stir. Cook for a further minute. Season with salt and pepper.
2. Add the cauliflower and cover the pan. Cook over a low heat for about 20 minutes, or until the cauliflower is cooked. Stir occasionally, adding more water if the mixture becomes too dry.
3. Serve sprinkled with the garam masala and lemon juice.

'FRIED' ONIONS

SERVES 4

PER PORTION Energy: 151kj/36kcal
Fat: 0.2g Saturated fat: trace

2 large onions, finely sliced

1. Put the onions into a very heavy saucepan. Add enough water to just cover. Simmer very slowly until all the water has evaporated.
2. Increase the temperature slightly and let the onions soften and brown. If they begin to burn, add a little water, let it evaporate, then continue the browning. Repeat this process until the onions are very soft and dark brown.

CURRIED BLACK-EYE BEANS

SERVES 4

PER PORTION Energy: 1109kj/265kcal
Fat: 5.5g Saturated fat: 0.5g

225g/8oz black-eye beans, soaked
  overnight and drained
1 tablespoon sunflower oil
2 onions, chopped
1 garlic clove, crushed
2.5cm/1 inch fresh ginger, grated
1 teaspoon ground cumin

2 teaspoons ground coriander
1 teaspoon ground turmeric
¼ teaspoon chilli powder
salt and freshly ground black pepper
1 tablespoon tomato purée
juice of ½ lemon
290ml/ ½ pint water
2 tablespoons chopped fresh coriander

1. Rinse the beans thoroughly and place in a large saucepan with plenty of water. Bring to the boil and boil rapidly for 10 minutes, uncovered.
2. Reduce the heat and simmer for 1 hour or until tender. Drain and keep covered until needed.
3. Heat the oil in a large saucepan and cook the onions over a low heat for 5–10 minutes, or until beginning to soften but not coloured.
4. Add the garlic and ginger and cook for a further 2 minutes. Add the cumin, coriander, turmeric, chilli powder and black pepper and cook for a further minute.
5. Add the beans, tomato purée, lemon juice and water and cook for a further 20 minutes. Taste and season with salt, if necessary.
6. Stir in the chopped coriander just before serving.

HOT PUDDINGS

HOT PUDDINGS

STEAMED FRUIT PARCELS

SERVES 4

PER PORTION Energy: 559kj/133kcal
Fat: 0.4g Saturated fat: trace

2 bananas
2 oranges
4 greengages
4 Victoria plums
1 William pear
small punnet of raspberries
1 tablespoon Cointreau
4 sheets tin foil, about 25cm/10 inches
* square*
mint leaves

1. Peel the bananas and cut into chunks. Peel each orange with a knife as you would an apple, making sure that all the pith is removed. Cut the oranges into segments: do this on a plate and reserve the juice. Halve and stone the greengages and plums. Peel, quarter and core the pear. Cut each quarter in half lengthways. Check over the raspberries.
2. Divide the fruit between the four squares of tin foil. Put the fruit in the centre of the foil and sprinkle with the reserved orange juice, Cointreau and mint leaves.

3. Fold up the edges of the foil to form sealed parcels and steam for 10 minutes. Serve immediately on individual plates.

NOTE: If no steamer is available, place the parcels on a preheated baking sheet and bake at 190°C/375°F/gas mark 5 for 7 minutes.

SPICED STEAMED PEARS WITH GRAPE SAUCE

SERVES 4

PER PORTION Energy: 468kj/111kcal
Fat: 0.4g Saturated fat: trace

4 pears
24 whole cloves
425ml/¾ pint white grape juice
grated zest of ½ lemon
grated nutmeg

1. Peel and halve the pears, then carefully remove the cores without breaking the flesh.
2. Stud the rounded side of each pear half with 3 cloves.
3. Put the grape juice into the bottom half of a steamer. Bring to the boil.
4. Place the top half of the steamer over the grape juice, add the pears and sprinkle with the lemon zest and grated nutmeg.
5. Steam until the pears are soft. This may take anything from 20 minutes to 1 hour, depending on how ripe the pears are. If they are very unripe, it may be necessary to add a little water to the grape juice; check it every so often to ensure that it is not beginning to caramelize.
6. Arrange the pears in a glass bowl, remove the cloves, then pour the reduced grape juice over the pears.

PEARS IN CIDER

SERVES 4

PER PORTION Energy: 460kj/110kcal
Fat: 0.2g Saturated fat: trace

4 large pears
290ml/½ pint medium-dry cider
30g/1oz caster sugar
3 cloves
1 cinnamon stick

To serve:
Low-fat natural yoghurt

1. Peel the pears and place in a saucepan with all the other ingredients and simmer for 1 hour, turning the pears halfway through cooking. They should remain firm but tender. Leave to cool slightly.
2. Remove the cloves and cinnamon and serve with low-fat natural yoghurt.

BAKED EXOTIC FRUITS

SERVES 6

PER PORTION Energy: 534kj/127kcal
Fat: 0.4g Saturated fat: trace

400ml/14oz tin lychees, drained and
* juice reserved*
1 mango, peeled and sliced
20 strawberries, hulled
110g/4oz blueberries
110g/4oz raspberries
pulp and juice of 8 passion-fruit
grated zest of 1 lime
2 tablespoons kirsch (optional)

For the syrup:
1 clove
grated zest and juice of 1 lime
1 vanilla pod, split open
1 cm/½ inch fresh ginger, grated
1 sprig rosemary
1 star anise

1. Set the oven to 240°C/475°F/gas
mark 8.
2. Mix the fruit and lime zest together
carefully, place in an ovenproof dish
and set aside.
3. Bring the lychee juice and syrup
ingredients to the boil and reduce, by
boiling rapidly, to a syrupy consistency.
4. Pour the syrup over the fruits, drizzle
with the kirsch (if using), cover with a
lid or foil and bake for 7 minutes. Serve
hot.

BAKED APPLES WITH MANGO AND BLUEBERRIES

SERVES 4

PER PORTION Energy: 956kj/228kcal
Fat: 0.4g Saturated fat: trace

4 medium cooking apples
1 ripe mango
110g/4oz blueberries
pinch ground cinnamon
2 tablespoons rum, or crème de cassis
* (optional)*
5mm/¼ inch water
15g/½oz light brown sugar

1. Heat the oven to 180°C/350°F/gas
mark 4.
2. Wash the apples and remove the
cores with an apple corer. With a sharp
knife, make an incision right round the
apple just through the skin about two-
thirds of the way up each fruit.
3. Peel the mango, cut into chunks, then
mix with the blueberries and cinnamon.
4. Put the apples into an ovenproof dish
and stuff the centres with the chopped
mango and blueberries.
5. Sprinkle with the rum or crème de
cassis, if using, and a little sugar. Then
pour 5mm/¼ inch water into the dish.
6. Bake in the oven for about 45
minutes, or until the apples are soft
right through when tested with a
skewer.

BANANAS BAKED WITH ORANGE, LYCHEE AND GINGER

SERVES 4

PER PORTION Energy: 928kj/221kcal Fat: 0.4g Saturated fat: 0.1g

4 ripe bananas
2 oranges, segmented
400ml/14oz tin lychees, strained and
  syrup reserved
2 preserved stem ginger, chopped
2 tablespoons syrup from ginger jar
1–3 tablespoons lemon juice

1. Set the oven to 180°C/350°F/gas mark 4.
2. Peel and halve the bananas lengthways, then arrange in an ovenproof dish with the orange segments. Scatter the lychees and stem ginger over them.
3. Pour the lychee syrup, ginger syrup and lemon juice on top. Ensure the bananas are completely covered by syrup or oranges, or if necessary cover with damp greaseproof paper – this helps prevent discoloration.
4. Bake in the oven for 20 minutes, or until the bananas are tender when tested with a skewer.

GRILLED PINEAPPLE AND MANGO SKEWERS

SERVES 4

PER SKEWER Energy: 436kj/104kcal Fat: 0.3g Saturated fat: trace

1 pineapple, peeled and cored
2 mangoes, peeled and stoned
2 tablespoons light muscovado sugar
2 tablespoons dark rum (optional)

1. Soak 8 wooden skewers in water for 1 hour or overnight.
2. Heat the grill to its highest setting.
3. Cut the pineapple and mangoes into 2.5cm/1 inch cubes, thread on to 8 skewers and arrange on a baking sheet.
4. Scatter with the sugar and drizzle with the rum.
5. Place under the grill and cook until the sugar caramelizes, basting with any juices. Serve immediately.

FIGS AND NECTARINES IN WINE WITH RASPBERRIES

SERVES 4

PER PORTION Energy: 663kj/158kcal Fat: 0.5g Saturated fat: trace

150ml/¼ pint water
290ml/½ pint muscat wine
pared zest of 1 lemon
1 cinnamon stick
4 ripe nectarines, stoned and cut into eighths
4 large figs, cut down to stem in quarters
225g/8oz raspberries

1. Place the water, wine, lemon zest and cinnamon in a heavy-bottomed saucepan and heat gently.
2. Place the nectarines in the pan. The fruit should be completely covered by the wine and water mixture, so choose a tall narrow pan. If this is not possible, wet the fruit in the mixture thoroughly and turn during cooking.
3. Bring the mixture to the boil slowly, then simmer for 7 minutes. Add the figs and cook for a further 7 minutes, or until the fruit looks glassy and is very tender.
4. Lift the fruit from the pan with a slotted spoon, and place in a bowl. Sprinkle with the raspberries.
5. Reduce the wine to a syrupy consistency by boiling rapidly, then strain over the fruits. Serve warm.

PLUMS AND VINE FRUITS WITH VANILLA

SERVES 4

PER PORTION Energy: 673kj/160kcal Fat: 0.2g Saturated fat: 0.1g

85g/3oz sultanas
2 tablespoons port
8 ripe plums
1 vanilla pod
1 bay leaf
30g/1oz demarara sugar
2 tablespoon water
225g/8oz seedless pink grapes
vanilla essence

To serve:
3 amaretti biscuits, crushed (optional)

1. Soak the sultanas in the port for 2 hours or overnight.
2. Set the oven to 170°C/325°F/gas mark 3.
3. Wash the plums, cut in half and remove the stones. Put them in a saucepan with the soaked sultanas, port, vanilla pod, sugar and 2 tablespoons water and bring to the boil. Reduce to a simmer and cook gently for 10–15 minutes, or until the fruit is tender. Add the grapes and cook for a further 5 minutes, or until soft. Stir in the vanilla essence.
4. To serve, remove the vanilla pod and bay leaf, scatter the fruit with the crushed amaretti, if using, and serve warm.

GRILLED PEACHES WITH BUTTERSCOTCH AND WHISKY SAUCE

SERVES 4

PER PORTION Energy: 707kj/169kcal
Fat: 1.6g Saturated fat: 0.9g

6 peaches
85g/3oz caster sugar
2 tablespoons single cream
2 tablespoons whisky

1. Set the oven to 190°C/375°F/gas mark 5.
2. Preheat the grill.
3. Cut the peaches in half and remove the stone.
4. Place the peaches in a shallow ovenproof dish, cut side down, and grill until very lightly charred.
5. Mix together the sugar, cream and whisky and pour over the peaches. Bake for 15 minutes, or until the peaches are soft. Turn the fruit once during cooking. Serve hot or cold.

APRICOT STRUDEL

SERVES 6

PER PORTION Energy: 1577kj/377kcal
Fat: 8.3g Saturated fat: 2.1g

450g/1lb ready-to-eat dried apricots
2 tablespoons amaretti liqueur
5 amaretti biscuits, crushed
225g/8oz filo pastry
2 tablespoons sunflower oil
icing sugar

To serve:
fresh raspberries

1. Place the apricots in a saucepan and just cover with water. Simmer for 15 minutes or until soft, then leave to cool.
2. Place the apricots and liqueur in a food processor or blender and liquidize. Mix with the amaretti biscuits.
3. Preheat the oven to 190°C/375°F/gas mark 5.
4. Carefully unfold the filo pastry and keep it covered with a damp tea towel to ensure that it does not dry out while you are working. Lift off one sheet and place it on a clean surface. Brush lightly with the oil and overlap by 2.5cm/1 inch with another sheet of filo pastry to form a large square. Continue this process until you have used up all the filo pastry.
5. Spread the pastry with the apricot mixture and roll up. Lightly brush the seam with the oil, bend the strudel into a horseshoe shape and place seam side down on a baking tray. Brush with the remaining oil.
6. Bake for 30–35 minutes, or until golden brown.
7. Dust with icing sugar and serve with raspberries.

COLD PUDDINGS

COLD PUDDINGS

STRAWBERRY AND ROSEMARY SORBET

SERVES 4

PER PORTION Energy: 830kj/198kcal
Fat: 0.1g Saturated fat: trace

5 large sprigs rosemary
170g/6oz caster sugar
570ml/1 pint water
juice of ½ lemon
340g/12oz fresh strawberries, hulled
2 egg whites

1. Place the rosemary sprigs, sugar and water in a heavy-bottomed saucepan and heat gently until the sugar has dissolved. When clear, boil gently for 5 minutes. Add the lemon and leave to cool for 30 minutes.
2. Liquidize or mash the strawberries to a pulp. Push through a sieve to remove large seeds.
3. Strain the cooled syrup into the strawberry purée and stir well. Put in a container and freeze for 30 minutes, or until the syrup is beginning to solidify.
4. When nearly frozen, return the sorbet to the liquidizer or food processor and whizz briefly. Gradually add the unwhisked egg white to the food processor: it will fluff up tremendously.

Taste and add more lemon if necessary. Return the mixture to the container and freeze until firm.

APRICOT AND ELDERFLOWER SORBET

SERVES 4

PER PORTION Energy: 1135kj/270kcal
Fat: 0.6g Saturated fat: 0.4g

55g/2oz caster sugar
290ml/½ pint water
340g/12oz dried unsulphured apricots
zest and juice of ½ lemon
200ml/7fl oz elderflower cordial
2 egg whites

1. Place the sugar, water, apricots and lemon zest in a heavy-bottomed saucepan and heat gently until the sugar has dissolved. When clear, boil gently for 5 minutes. Add the lemon juice and elderflower cordial. Cool and liquidize or process.
2. Put the apricot mixture into a bowl in the freezer for 30 minutes, or until the syrup is beginning to solidify.
3. Whisk the egg whites until stiff and fold into the half-frozen mixture. Return to the freezer until solid. Alternatively, when nearly frozen, briefly process or liquidize the sorbet again. Gradually add the unwhisked egg white to the food processor: it will fluff up tremendously. Return the mixture to the container and freeze until firm.

GOOSEBERRY AND ELDERFLOWER SORBET

SERVES 4

PER PORTION Energy: 552kj/132kcal
Fat: 0.5g Saturated fat: trace

450g/1lb gooseberries
100g/3½oz caster sugar
125ml/4fl oz water
2 tablespoons elderflower cordial
juice of 1 lemon
1 egg white

1. Top and tail the gooseberries. Process or liquidize the fruit, then sieve to remove the seeds.
2. Put the sugar, water and cordial into a saucepan and heat gently until the sugar has dissolved. Turn up the heat and boil fast for 5 minutes, or until a sticky syrup forms. Cool. When the syrup has cooled, add the gooseberry purée and lemon juice.
3. Place the mixture in a deep bowl in the freezer and leave until half-frozen.
4. Whisk the egg white until stiff but not dry and fold into the gooseberry mixture. Return the mixture to the freezer. Alternatively, when nearly frozen, briefly process or liquidize the sorbet again. Gradually add the unwhisked egg white to the food processor: it will fluff up tremendously. Return to the container and freeze until firm. Remove the sorbet 10–15 minutes before serving.

HONEY AND ROSEMARY PARFAIT

SERVES 4

PER PORTION Energy: 728kj/173kcal
Fat: 0.8g Saturated fat: 0.5g

150ml/¼ pint clear runny honey
4 sprigs rosemary
zest of ½ lemon
4 tablespoons water
3 egg whites
425ml/¾ pint natural yoghurt

1. In a small saucepan mix the honey, rosemary, lemon zest and 4 tablespoons water. Leave for 30 minutes to infuse.
2. Heat the mixture gently until the honey has dissolved, then bring to the boil. Boil for 5 minutes or until 'tacky'. Strain and set aside.
3. In a medium-sized bowl whisk the egg whites to stiff peaks.
4. Pour the hot syrup on to the egg whites in a steady stream while whisking constantly (take care not to pour the syrup on to the wires of the whisk – it may cool too fast on the cold metal).
5. Continue whisking until the mixture is stiff and shiny and absolutely stable and cold. If the whisk is lifted, the meringue should not flow.
6. Fold in the yoghurt, put into a container and freeze.
7. When half-frozen, whisk again or whizz in a food processor, then return to the freezer.

STRAWBERRY, RASPBERRY AND CARDAMOM GRANITA

The ideal granita has an even but grainy consistency which can only be achieved by manual stirring with a fork. If you prefer to use a mechanical process, follow step 4 in the strawberry and rosemary sorbet (see page 213) rather than step 4 below. This will produce a sorbet rather than a granita.

SERVES 4

PER PORTION Energy: 727kj/173kcal
Fat: 0.2g Saturated fat: trace

*5 cardamom pods, seeds removed and
    crushed*
145g/5oz granulated sugar
570ml/1 pint water
juice of ½ lemon
170g/6oz fresh strawberries
170g/6oz fresh raspberries
*2 egg whites (if making a sorbet, see
    above)*

1. Place the cardamom, sugar and water in a heavy-bottomed saucepan and heat gently until the sugar has dissolved. When clear, boil gently for 5 minutes. Add the lemon juice and leave to cool.
2. Liquidize or mash the strawberries and raspberries to a pulp. Push through a sieve to remove the seeds.
3. Strain the cooled syrup into the purée and stir well. Put in a shallow container and freeze for 30 minutes, or until the purée is beginning to solidify at the edges, about 1 hour.
4. Stir the purée with a fork to mix the ice crystals evenly. Return to the freezer until the purée is again beginning to solidify at the edges.
5. Repeat this stirring process two or three times, or until the mixture has an even consistency of small ice crystals. It should be grainy but not mushy. Serve as soon as possible.
6. If the granita is to be kept overnight, remove it from the freezer 2 hours before serving and allow to soften for 30 minutes. Stir thoroughly with a fork and return to the freezer. After 30 minutes, stir the purée once more and refreeze.

SEMI-FROZEN RED FRUITS

SERVES 4

PER PORTION Energy: 471kj/112kcal
Fat: 0.5g Saturated fat: trace

225g/8oz strawberries, hulled
225g/8oz raspberries
2 tablespoons crème de cassis
1 mango
110g/4oz blueberries
2 cardamom pods, seeds removed and
  crushed

To serve:
light Greek yoghurt

1. Pick out half of the softer strawberries and raspberries and mash with a fork. Push through a sieve, then add the crème de cassis.
2. Peel and chop the mango and halve the larger strawberries, mix all the fruits together in a bowl, add the crushed cardamom and stir well. Stir in the red fruit sauce, place the mixture in a container and freeze for about 1 hour, or until crystals start to form.
3. When half-frozen, stir gently, then return to the freezer for another hour. Repeat this procedure once more. The process takes about 2 hours. Do not allow the mixture to freeze completely. Serve semi-frozen with the Greek yoghurt.

RHUBARB AND ORANGE TERRINE

SERVES 8

PER PORTION Energy: 709kj/169kcal
Fat: 3.8g Saturated fat: 2.0g

675g/1½lb trimmed rhubarb
85g/3oz granulated sugar
4 tablespoons water
30g/1oz gelatine
2 oranges
200g/7oz medium-fat soft cheese
1 egg, separated
2 pieces stem ginger, finely chopped
55g/2oz caster sugar

For the garnish:
2 oranges, segmented

1. Cut the rhubarb into 2.5cm/1 inch lengths, place in a saucepan and sprinkle with granulated sugar. Add 1 tablespoon water and stew very gently for 10–15 minutes or until tender. Cool and liquidize or process.
2. Put the remaining water in a small saucepan and sprinkle in 20g/¾oz of the gelatine. Leave to stand for 5 minutes, then heat gently until dissolved. When clear and liquid, mix with the rhubarb. Add the juice from 1 orange and leave to cool, stirring occasionally.
3. Beat the cheese and the egg yolk. Add the ginger and beat again.
4. Grate the zest of the remaining orange and add to the cheese mixture. Squeeze the orange and place the juice in a small saucepan. Sprinkle in the remaining gelatine, leave to stand for 5 minutes, then heat gently until dissolved. When liquid, miv with the cheese mixture and stir until nearly at the point of setting.
5. Whisk the egg white until fairly stiff. Add the caster sugar 1 tablespoon at a time and continue to whisk for another 30 seconds. Fold into the cheese mixture.
6. Line the base of a 450g/1lb loaf tin with lightly oiled greaseproof paper. When the cheese and rhubarb mixtures are nearly set, put alternate layers of them in the tin, starting and finishing with a layer of the cheese mixture. Leave to set in the refrigerator for 2–3 hours, then turn out. Garnish with the orange segments.

ELDERFLOWER AND YOGHURT JELLY

SERVES 6

PER PORTION Energy: 459kj/109kcal
Fat: 0.4g Saturated fat: 0.3g

250ml/9fl oz elderflower cordial
20g/¾oz gelatine
grated zest of ½ lemon
250ml/9fl oz low-fat fromage frais
250ml/9fl oz natural yoghurt
2 egg whites

To serve:
fresh grapes and/or apricot sauce (see
  page 229)

1. Put half the elderflower cordial into a small saucepan. Sprinkle in the gelatine and allow to stand for 10 minutes. Heat gently, without boiling or stirring, until the gelatine has dissolved. When the gelatine is clear and liquid, remove from the heat.
2. Put the lemon zest into the remaining cordial and leave to stand for 10 minutes. Remove the zest, then mix the cordial with the fromage frais and yoghurt. Stir well to remove any lumps. Pour in the gelatine mixture, combine well and cool. Stir gently until the mixture is on the point of setting.
3. In a clean bowl whisk the egg whites until medium peak, then fold carefully into the elderflower mixture.
4. Line a 1 litre/1¾ pint terrine or plain jelly mould with cling film and pour in the elderflower mixture. Cover and chill in the refrigerator for 2–4 hours, or until set.
5. When ready to serve, loosen the jelly around the edge. Invert a serving plate over the mould, turn mould and plate over together, give a sharp shake and remove the mould. Peel away all the cling film. Decorate with the grapes and/or apricot sauce.

PASSION-FRUIT AND MANGO JELLY

SERVES 4

PER PORTION Energy: 520kj/124kcal
Fat: 0.4g Saturated fat: trace

6 ripe passion-fruit
290ml/ ½ pint orange juice
3 tablespoons water
15g/ ½oz gelatine
1–3 tablespoons icing sugar (to taste)
1 ripe mango, peeled and cut into chunks

For the garnish:
110g/4oz strawberries

1. Sieve the passion-fruit pulp to remove the seeds, if desired, and mix with the orange juice.
2. Put 3 tablespoons water into a small saucepan, sprinkle in the gelatine and allow to stand for 5 minutes. Heat gently, without boiling or stirring, until the gelatine has dissolved.
3. When the gelatine is clear and liquid, remove from the heat and pour into the passion-fruit mixture. Taste and add sugar, mixed with a little water, if necessary.
4. Place the mango chunks in a wet plain jelly mould. Pour in three-quarters of the passion-fruit mixture. Refrigerate until beginning to solidify, then pour in the remaining liquid. This ensures that the jelly has a flat bottom when turned out. Return to the refrigerator until set, about 4 hours.

5. To serve: dip the outside of the mould into a bowl of hot water for a couple of seconds. Invert a serving plate over the mould, turn mould and plate over together, give a sharp shake and remove the mould. Garnish with the strawberries.

APPLE JELLY WITH GREEN FRUITS

SERVES 4

PER PORTION Energy: 395kj/94kcal
Fat: 0.3g Saturated fat: trace

425ml/¾ pint clear apple juice
20g/¾oz gelatine
1 small melon, with green flesh
110g/4oz green grapes

1. Put 6 tablespoons of the apple juice into a small saucepan. Sprinkle in the gelatine and allow to stand for 10 minutes. Heat gently, without boiling or stirring, until the gelatine has dissolved.
2. When the gelatine is liquid, mix with the remaining apple juice and pour a layer about 1cm/½ inch deep in the bottom of a clean 860ml/1½ pint jelly mould. Place in the refrigerator to set.
3. Using a melon baller, scoop the melon flesh into balls, or simply cut into even-sized cubes. Halve and deseed the grapes.
4. When the jelly in the mould has set, sprinkle in the fruit, then pour in enough apple liquid to make the fruit start to move. Return to the refrigerator. When this layer has set, pour in apple liquid to reach the top of the mould and return to the refrigerator.
5. To turn out the jelly, dip the outside of the mould briefly in hot water. Invert a wet plate over the mould and turn both over together. Give a sharp shake and remove the mould.

GRAPE JELLY WITH MELON AND PLUMS

SERVES 4

PER PORTION Energy: 442kj/105kcal
Fat: 0.2g Saturated fat: trace

425ml/¾ pint clear red grape juice
20g/¾oz gelatine
1 small melon, with orange flesh
110g/4oz ripe pink grapes
1 ripe red plum

1. Put 6 tablespoons of the grape juice in a small saucepan. Sprinkle in the gelatine and allow to stand for 10 minutes. Heat gently, without boiling or stirring, until the gelatine has dissolved.
2. When the gelatine is clear and liquid, mix with the remaining grape juice and pour a layer about 1cm/½ inch deep in the bottom of a clean 860ml/1½ pint jelly mould. Place in the refrigerator to set.
3. Using a melon baller, scoop the melon flesh into balls, or simply cut into even-sized cubes. Halve and deseed the grapes. Stone and chop the plum.
4. When the jelly in the mould has set, sprinkle in the fruit, pour in enough grape liquid to make the fruit start to move, then return to the refrigerator. When this layer has set, pour in enough grape liquid to reach the top of the mould and return to the refrigerator.
5. To turn out the jelly, dip the outside of the mould briefly in a bowl of hot water. Invert a wet plate over the mould and turn both over together. Give a sharp shake and remove the mould.

STRIPED FRUIT JELLY

SERVES 8

PER PORTION Energy: 496kj/118kcal
Fat: 0.4g Saturated fat: 0.4g

130ml/4fl oz apple juice
30g/1oz gelatine
2 mangoes, peeled and stoned
2 passion-fruit
450g/1lb strawberries, hulled
170g/6oz raspberries
1 melon with green flesh
icing sugar, to taste
squeeze of lemon juice

For the garnish:
raspberries
strawberries
mint leaves

1. Put the apple juice into a small saucepan. Sprinkle in the gelatine and allow to stand for 10 minutes.
2. Process or liquidize the mango flesh and passion-fruit pulp until smooth. Set aside in a bowl.
3. Put the strawberries into the cleaned food processor, reduce to a purée, then push through a sieve. Mix in the whole raspberries and set aside in a bowl.
4. Peel and deseed the melon, put the flesh into the cleaned food processor and reduce to a purée. Set aside in a bowl.
5. Taste all three purées, adding icing sugar to sweeten or lemon juice to give a 'bite'. Leave to stand until the froth

made by the processor subsides.
6. Gently heat the gelatine, without boiling or stirring until dissolved.
7. When the gelatine is clear and liquid, remove from the heat and pour 2 tablespoons into the warm mango and passion-fruit purée, 3 tablespoons into the warm strawberry purée and 4 tablespoons into the melon purée.
8. Pour the mango and passion-fruit purée into a wet jelly mould and refrigerate until beginning to set. Then pour in the strawberry and raspberry purée and refrigerate until set. Finally, pour in the melon purée and refrigerate for 2–3 hours, until set.
9. To serve: Dip the outside of the mould briefly into a bowl of hot water. Invert a wet plate over the mould and turn both over together. Give a sharp shake and remove the mould.
10. Garnish with raspberries, strawberries and mint leaves.

APPLE AND QUINCE MOUSSE

SERVES 4

PER PORTION Energy: 510kj/121kcal
Fat: 0.4g Saturated fat: 0.2g

2 Bramley apples, peeled and cored
2 quinces, peeled and cored
zest of 1 orange
4 tablespoons water
30–55g/1–2oz sugar
2 tablespoons calvados (optional)
15g/½oz gelatine
150ml/¼ pint low-fat yoghurt
lemon juice to taste
honey, to taste
2 egg whites

1. Peel and core the apples and quinces. Cut them into chunks. Put them, with the orange zest and 4 tablespoons water, into a heavy-bottomed saucepan, cover and simmer gently until they are a soft pulp. Remove the lid, add the sugar and boil, stirring constantly, until you have a stiffish purée. Remove from the heat and stir in the calvados, if using. Remove the orange zest and leave to cool.
2. Process or liquidize the mixture until very smooth.
3. In a small pan soak the gelatine in 3 tablespoons water for 10 minutes.
4. Dissolve the gelatine over a gentle heat and, when clear and warm, add it to the purée. Stir gently until the mixture is on the point of setting, then fold in the yoghurt. Taste: if too bland, add a squeeze of lemon juice; if too tart, stir in a little honey.
5. Whisk the egg whites into medium peaks and fold into the mousse with a large metal spoon.
6. Pour the mixture into a soufflé dish and leave to set in the refrigerator for 2–3 hours.

PEAR AND ORANGE PUDDING

SERVES 4

PER PORTION Energy: 583kj/139kcal
Fat: 0.2g Saturated fat: trace

900g/2lb ripe pears
pared zest and juice of 1 large orange
pinch ground ginger
4 tablespoons Cointreau
icing sugar, to taste
lemon juice, to taste
2 egg whites

1. Peel and core the pears. Cut them into chunks and place in a saucepan with the orange juice, zest and ginger. Cover and simmer gently until soft. Beat out any lumps with a wooden spoon. Liquidize or process, if necessary.
2. If the purée is very sloppy, boil it rapidly to reduce and thicken, but leave the lid on as it splashes dangerously.
3. Add the Cointreau and leave to cool.
4. When the purée is completely cold, remove the orange zest, then taste and add icing sugar and/or lemon juice, as necessary. The purée should be strongly flavoured as the egg whites will dilute it.
5. Whisk the egg whites into medium peaks and fold into the purée with a large metal spoon. Pour the mixture into individual glasses or a serving dish and chill in the refrigerator.

NOTE: After the egg whites have been folded into the mixture, the pudding will hold for only a few hours.

SUMMER FRUITS WITH WHITE CHEESE

SERVES 4

PER PORTION Energy: 732kj/174kcal
Fat: 3.0g Saturated fat: 1.6g

225g/8oz cottage cheese
2 cardamom pods, seeds removed and
  crushed
150ml/¼ pint natural yoghurt, lightly
  beaten
vanilla essence
110g/4oz strawberries
110g/4oz blueberries
1 mango, peeled and diced
110g/4oz raspberries

For the raspberry purée:
225g/8oz raspberries
icing sugar to taste

For the garnish:
4 sprigs mint

1. Place the cottage cheese in a sieve and
drain very well.
2. Make the raspberry purée by
liquidizing the raspberries with enough
water to make a smooth sauce. Taste
and add a little sugar to sweeten, if
required. Strain and set aside.
3. Push the cottage cheese with the
crushed cardamom seeds through a
sieve or process briefly in a processor.
Fold in the yoghurt, add 2 drops vanilla
essence and sweeten if desired. Chill.
4. To serve: pour the raspberry sauce on
to one side of four pudding plates. Put a
spoonful of the cheese mixture on the
other side. Add the fruits and garnish
with mint.

CITRUS AND CRANBERRY FRUIT SALAD

SERVES 4

PER PORTION Energy: 421kj/100kcal
Fat: 0.3g Saturated fat: trace

110g/4oz cranberries
2 tablespoons honey
½ teaspoon ground cardamom
1 pink grapefruit
2 oranges
2 passion-fruit
1 teaspoon orange flower water
(optional)
1 tablespoon kirsch (optional)

For the garnish:
mint leaves

1. In a small saucepan cook the cranberries with the honey and cardamom until just soft. Allow to cool.
2. Peel the grapefruit and oranges with a sharp knife, as you would an apple, removing all the pith. Cut out the individual segments, leaving behind the membranes. Tip into a bowl and add the passion-fruit pulp and seeds.
3. When the cranberries are cool, mix all the ingredients, plus the orange flower water and kirsch (if using), transfer into a serving bowl and garnish with the fresh mint leaves.

SPICED MANGO AND PAPAYA SALAD

While this is a delicious pudding, it can also make a refreshing first course in the summer or a side dish with cold meats.

SERVES 4

PER PORTION Energy: 518kj/123kcal
Fat: 0.3g Saturated fat: trace

1 mango
1 papaya
1 × 400g/14oz tin lychees, or 12 fresh
lychees
2 tablespoons Cointreau
zest and juice of 1 lime
½ green chilli, very finely chopped (see
page 91)

1. Peel, deseed and thinly slice the mango and papaya. Skin and stone the lychees, if using fresh ones.
2. Arrange all the fruit on a large plate. Mix together the Cointreau, lime zest, lime juice and chilli and pour over the fruits. Cover, refrigerate and leave to macerate for 2 hours.

SWEET SAUCES

SWEET SAUCES

APRICOT SAUCE

SERVES 4

PER PORTION Energy: 256kj/56kcal
Fat: 0.2g Saturated fat: 0.1g

110g/4oz dried apricots, soaked
  overnight
110g/4oz tinned apricots in natural juice
570ml/1 pint water

1. Drain the dried apricots and put them
into a saucepan with the tinned apricots
and water. Bring to the boil and simmer
until tender.
2. Liquidize and then push through a
sieve. If the sauce is too thin, reduce it
by rapid boiling to the required
consistency. If it is too thick, add a little
water.

NOTE: This sauce can be served hot or
cold.

RASPBERRY COULIS

SERVES 4

PER PORTION Energy: 90kj/21kcal
Fat: 0.3g Saturated fat: trace

340g/12oz fresh raspberries
juice of ½ lemon

1. Process or liquidize the ingredients
together, then push through a conical
strainer.

NOTE: If the sauce is too thin, it can be
thickened by boiling rapidly in a heavy
saucepan. Stir well to prevent it
'catching'.

MANGO COULIS

SERVES 4

PER PORTION Energy: 480kj/114kcal
Fat: 0.4g Saturated fat: trace

*2 mangoes, peeled, stoned and cut into
    large chunks
juice of ½ lemon*

1. Process or liquidize the ingredients
together until smooth, then push
through a sieve.

APPLE PURÉE

SERVES 4

PER PORTION Energy: 350kj/83kcal
Fat: 0.1g Saturated fat: trace

*450g/1lb cooking apples
55g/2oz sugar
4 tablespoons water*

1. Peel and core the apples. Cut them
into chunks. Put them with the sugar
and water in a heavy saucepan and
simmer gently until they become a soft
pulp. Beat out any lumps with a
wooden spoon.
2. If the purée is too sloppy, boil it
rapidly to reduce and thicken it, but
leave the lid half on as it splashes
dangerously.

SWEET GOOSEBERRY SAUCE

SERVES 4

PER PORTION Energy: 449kj/107kcal
Fat: 0.2g Saturated fat: trace

*225g/8oz ripe gooseberries
150ml/¼ pint water
85g/3oz sugar
pinch ground ginger*

1. Put all the ingredients in a thick-
bottomed saucepan. Bring gradually to
the boil, then simmer until the
gooseberries pop open and change to a
yellowish colour.
2. Push through a sieve and reheat.

MELBA SAUCE

SERVES 4

PER PORTION Energy: 162kj/39kcal
Fat: 0.2g Saturated fat: trace

*225g/8oz fresh or frozen (not tinned)
    raspberries
icing sugar*

1. Defrost the raspberries if frozen. Push
them through a nylon or stainless sieve
to remove all seeds.
2. Sift in icing sugar to taste. If too
thick, add a few spoonfuls of water.

BREADS AND TOAST

BREADS AND TOAST

WHITE BREAD

PER LOAF Energy: 7381kj/1757kcal
Fat: 28.4g Saturated fat: 3.8g

You will need a 1kg/2lb loaf tin. If it is
old and used, you may not need to
grease or flour it, but if it is new and not
non-stick, brush it out very lightly with
flavourless oil and dust with flour.

It using dried yeast, one 7g/¼oz easy-
blend sachet usually equals 15g/½oz
conventional dried yeast or 30g/1oz
fresh yeast. Easy-blend yeast is mixed
directly with the flour, not reconstituted
in liquid first.

To make flavoured breads, see
variations at the end of this recipe.

15g/½oz fresh yeast
290ml/½ pint warm water
450g/1lb strong flour
1 teaspoon salt
2 tablespoons sunflower oil
extra flour to dust, or milk to brush
½ tablespoon poppy or sesame seeds.

1. Dissolve the fresh yeast with a little
of the water in a small bowl.
2. Sift the flour with the salt into a large
bowl and make a well in the centre.
Pour in the yeast mixture, the remaining
water and the oil and mix to a softish
dough.

3. Add a small amount of flour if the
dough is too sticky. When the dough
will leave the sides of the bowl, press it
into a ball and tip out on to a floured
board.
4. Knead until it is elastic, smooth and
shiny, about 15 minutes.
5. Put the dough in a lightly oiled bowl,
cover it with oiled polythene and leave
somewhere warm and draught-free to
rise and double in size. This should take
at least 1 hour. Bread that rises too
quickly has a yeasty, unpleasant taste;
the slower the rising the better –
overnight in a cool larder is better than
half an hour on the boiler!
6. When ready, knead for a further 10
minutes or so and add any flavourings
you might be using.
7. Shape the dough into an oblong and
put it into the loaf tin.
8. Cover with oiled polythene and allow
to rise again until it is the size and shape
of a loaf, or one and a half times its
original size.
9. Set the oven to 200°C/400°F/gas
mark 6.
10. Sift a little flour over the loaf, or
brush with milk and scatter with poppy
or sesame seeds. Bake in the oven for
25–30 minutes, or until golden and firm.
It should sound hollow when tapped on
the underside. If it does not, or feels
squashy and heavy, return it to the

oven, without the tin, for a further 10 minutes.

11. Turn the loaf out on to a wire rack to cool.

VARIATIONS: To flavour the bread, add any one of the following at step 6.

- *1 tablespoon dry roasted fennel, caraway or cumin seeds*
- *2 tablespoons dry-roasted pinenuts, sesame, sunflower or pumpkin seeds*
- *2 tablespoons chopped hazelnuts, pecans, cashews or walnuts*
- *2 tablespoons chopped thyme or rosemary*
- *1 tablespoon chopped olives or sun-dried tomatoes*
- *2 tablespoons mixed nuts and dried fruits*

NOTE: Adding nuts, seeds, dried fruit, olives or sun-dried tomatoes will slightly alter the nutritional analysis.

ITALIAN BREAD

PER LOAF Energy: 692kj/1649kcal
Fat: 17.0g Saturated fat: 2.3g

This is a basic olive oil bread which can be adapted easily by adding a variety of herbs such as rosemary or sage (see left).

30g/1oz fresh yeast (see Note)
225ml/8fl oz warm water
450g/1lb plain flour
2 teaspoons salt
1 tablespoon olive oil

1. Dissolve the yeast in the warm water.
2. Sift the flour and salt on to a work surface and make a well in the centre. Pour in the dissolved yeast and olive oil. Gradually draw in the flour and when all the ingredients are well mixed, knead the dough for 8 minutes.
3. Put the dough in a lightly floured bowl. Cover with a damp tea towel and leave to rise in a warm place. This will take about 1 hour.
4. Shape as required and bake at 230°C/450°F/gas mark 8 for 10 minutes. Reduce the oven to 190°C/375°F/gas mark 5 and bake for about 45 minutes. Remove to a cooling rack and leave until completely cold.

NOTE: If using dried yeast or easy-blend yeast, see page 233.

BROWN SODA BREAD

Many soda bread recipes call for buttermilk, but we have found that it works well using ordinary milk.

8 SERVINGS Energy: 879kj/209kcal
Fat: 3.3g Saturated fat: 1.5g

*450g/1lb wholemeal flour, or 340g/12oz
   wholemeal flour and 110g/4oz plain
   white flour*
1 teaspoon salt
1 teaspoon bicarbonate of soda
2 teaspoons cream of tartar
1 teaspoon sugar
20g/¾oz butter
*290–435ml/½–¾ pint skimmed milk (if
   using all wholemeal flour, the recipe
   will need more liquid than if made
   with a mixture of 2 flours)*

1. Set the oven to 190°C/375°F/gas mark 5.
2. Sift the dry ingredients into a warm, dry bowl.
3. Rub in the butter and mix to a soft dough with the milk.
4. Shape with a minimum of kneading into a large circle about 5cm/2 inches thick. With the handle of a wooden spoon, make a cross on top of the loaf. The dent should be 2cm/¾ inch deep.
5. Bake on a greased baking sheet for 25–30 minutes. Allow to cool on a wire rack.

GRANARY BREAD

PER LOAF Energy: 6969kj/1659kcal
Fat: 30.1g Saturated fat: 4.0g

15g/½oz fresh yeast (see Note)
290ml/½ pint lukewarm water
450g/1lb granary flour
1 teaspoon salt
2 tablespoons sunflower oil

1. Dissolve the fresh yeast with a little of the water in a small bowl.
2. Sift the flour with the salt into a large bowl, returning the grains to the flour. Make a well in the centre, pour in the yeast mixture, the remaining water and the oil and mix to a softish dough.
3. Add a small amount of flour if the dough is too sticky. When the dough will leave the sides of the bowl, press it into a ball and tip on to a floured board.
4. Knead until it is elastic, smooth and shiny, about 15 minutes.
5. Put the dough in a lightly oiled bowl, cover with oiled polythene and leave somewhere warm and draught-free to rise and double in size. This should take at least 1 hour.
6. Brush a 1kg/2lb loaf tin lightly with oil and dust with flour.
7. When the dough is ready, knead it for a further 10 minutes or so, shape it into an oblong and place in the loaf tin.
8. Cover with oiled polythene and allow to rise again until it is the size and shape of a loaf, or one and a half times its own size.
9. Set the oven to 200°C/400°F/gas mark 6.

10. Sift a little flour over the loaf and bake in the oven for 25–30 minutes, or until it is firm and it sounds hollow when tapped on the underside.
11. Turn on to a wire rack to cool.

NOTE: If using dried yeast or easy-blend yeast, see page 233.

WHOLEMEAL BREAD

This wholemeal bread is simple to make as it has only one rising. As with all bread made from 100 per cent wholemeal flour, it will be heavier than bread made from a mixture of flours. The flour and water quantities are approximations as wholemeal flours vary enormously. The dough should be moist but not sticky. Use the smaller quantity called for and add extra flour or water as necessary.

MAKES 2 LOAVES

PER LOAF Energy: 3632kj/865kcal Fat: 6.2g Saturated fat: 0.9g

560g–615g/1lb 4oz–1lb 6oz stoneground wholemeal flour
1 teaspoon salt
3 tablespoons buttermilk
290–350ml/10–12fl oz warm water
15g/½oz fresh yeast (for dried yeast halve this quantity)

1. Warm the flour with the salt in a mixing bowl in the bottom of a low oven for about 5 minutes. Warm 2 × 675g/1½lb non-stick loaf tins.
2. Mix the buttermilk with the warm water. Add a little of the liquid to the yeast with a pinch of flour. If using dried yeast, set the mixture aside for 10 minutes. It is ready when frothy.
3. Make a well in the centre of the flour, pour in the yeast mixture and nearly all the water and buttermilk. Mix to a dough. Add extra flour or liquid as required. Knead well.
4. Fill the warmed tins three-quarters full of dough. Smooth the tops and cover with greased polythene. Leave in a warm place for 45 minutes, or until the dough has risen to the top of the tins.
5. While the dough is rising, preheat the oven to 225°C/450°F/gas mark 8.
6. Bake the bread for 15 minutes. Reduce the heat to 195°C/375°F/gas mark 5 and bake for a further 25 minutes.
7. The bread should sound hollow when it is tapped on the underside. If it does not, or feels squashy and heavy, return it to the oven, without the tin, for a further 5–10 minutes. Leave to cool on a wire rack.

BALLYMALOE BROWN BREAD

PER LOAF Energy: 6356kj/1513kcal
Fat: 18.7g Saturated fat: 2.6g

30g/1oz yeast
1 teaspoon black treacle
350–425ml/12–15fl oz water at blood
  heat
450g/1lb wholemeal flour
1 teaspoon salt
1 tablespoon sesame seeds

1. Grease a 13 × 20cm/5 × 8 inch loaf
tin.
2. Mix the yeast with the treacle and
150ml/¼ pint of the water, and leave in
a warm place for about 5 minutes, by
which time it should look creamy and
slightly frothy on top.
3. Sift the flour and salt into a large
bowl. Make a well in the centre and add
the yeast mixture and enough of the
remaining liquid to make a wettish
dough that would be just too wet to
knead.
4. Put the dough in the loaf tin and
smooth down the surface. Sprinkle with
the sesame seeds and pat down. Place
the tin in a warm place and cover with a
dry tea towel. Leave to rise for 15–30
minutes.
5. Preheat the oven to 230°C/470°F/gas
mark 9.
6. Place the bread in the hot oven for
45–50 minutes. After about 30 minutes,
remove the bread from the tin and
replace it in the oven to continue

cooking. When cooked, it should sound
hollow when tapped on the bottom.

NOTE: If using dried yeast or easy-blend
yeast, see page 233.

POTATO BREAD

MAKES 3 LOAVES

PER LOAF Energy: 3733kj/889kcal
Fat: 3.6g Saturated fat: 0.6g

*450g/1lb potatoes, peeled, cooked and
  mashed with milk*
30g/1oz yeast
425ml/¾ pint lukewarm water
675g/1½lb flour, preferably 'strong'
2 teaspoons salt

1. Allow the potatoes to cool until
lukewarm.
2. Dissolve the yeast in the lukewarm
water. Mix it with the mashed potatoes.
3. Sift the flour into a bowl with the
salt. Add the potato and yeast mixture
and mix well. When the mixture will
leave the sides of the bowl, press it into
a ball and tip it out on to a floured
surface.
4. Knead until it is elastic, smooth and
shiny; this will probably take 15
minutes.
5. Put the dough back in the bowl, cover
it with lightly greased polythene and
leave somewhere warm and draught-
free to rise and double in size. This
should take at least 1 hour.
6. When ready, knead for a further 10
minutes or so.
7. Shape into 3 loaves, cover with
polythene and leave to rise again for 15
minutes. Dust lightly with flour.
8. Preheat the oven to 220°C/425°F/gas
mark 7.

9. Bake the loaves for 10 minutes. Turn
the oven down to 190°C/375°F/gas
mark 5 and bake for a further 25
minutes, or until golden brown and
firm.
10. Turn out on to a wire rack to cool.
The bread should sound hollow when
tapped on the underside. If not, return
to the oven for a further few minutes.

NOTE: If using dried yeast or easy-blend
yeast, see page 233.

HAZELNUT AND RAISIN BREAD

MAKES 1 LOAF OR 10 ROLLS

PER LOAF Energy: 8191kj/1950kcal
Fat: 38.6g Saturated fat: 4.2g
PER ROLL Energy: 819kj/195kcal
Fat: 3.9g Saturated fat: 0.4g

225g/8oz *strong plain flour*
225g/8oz *wholemeal flour*
1 *teaspoon salt*
15g/½oz *fresh yeast or 7g/½oz dried yeast (see note)*
290ml/½ *pint lukewarm water*
1 *tablespoon olive oil*
55g/2oz *raisins*
30g/1oz *hazelnuts, toasted, skinned and roughly chopped*
extra flour for dusting

1. Sift the flours and salt into a mixing bowl and make a well in the centre.
2. Mix the yeast with 1 tablespoon warm water. Pour into the well with the rest of the water and oil.
3. Mix with a knife, then draw together with the fingers of one hand to make a soft but not sticky dough.
4. Knead until smooth and elastic, about 10 minutes, using more flour if necessary.
5. Put the dough into a large, clean and oiled bowl, cover with lightly greased polythene and leave in a warm place to rise until double in bulk, about 1 hour.
6. Heat the oven to 190°C/375°F/gas mark 5.

7. Knock back the dough and carefully knead the raisins and hazelnuts into it. Shape into a round or oval loaf, place on a baking sheet and make diagonal slashes at even intervals on top. Alternatively, divide into 10 pieces and shape into rolls.
8. Cover the loaf or rolls with lightly greased polythene and leave in a warm place until they have reached one and a half times their original size. Dust the top(s) with a little flour.
9. Place in the oven. Bake the loaf for 30 minutes, or until it sounds hollow when tapped on the underside; bake the rolls for 15–20 minutes.
10. Place on a wire rack to cool.

VARIATIONS: This recipe can easily be adapted to using other fruits and nuts. We suggest making a double quantity of dough and then adding ingredients of your choice at step 7. Suitable additions include dried apricots, peaches, pears, figs, cranberries, mango or prunes, and cashews, pecans, brazil nuts, walnuts or almonds. Some changes will slightly alter the nutritional analysis.

NOTE: If using dried yeast or easy-blend yeast, see page 233.

GARLIC BREAD

MAKES 2 LOAVES

PER PORTION Energy: 1075kj/256kcal
Fat: 6.3g Saturated fat: 0.9g

2 tablespoons olive oil
8 whole garlic cloves, unpeeled
15g/½oz fresh yeast
pinch sugar
150ml/¼ pint lukewarm water
225g/8oz plain flour
½ teaspoon salt

For the garnish:
1 tablespoon coarse sea salt (optional)

1. Heat the oil and garlic in a small pan over a low heat for 10 minutes. Do not boil or allow the garlic to brown. Remove from the heat and leave for 15 minutes to infuse and cool.
2. Cream the fresh yeast with the sugar and 2 tablespoons lukewarm water.
3. Sift the flour with the salt and make a well in the centre. Pour in the yeast mixture, the remaining water and 1 tablespoon of the oil. Mix together until it turns into a soft but not wet dough. Add more water or flour if necessary.
4. Turn out on to a floured surface and knead well for about 5 minutes until the dough is smooth. Place in a clean bowl, cover with greased polythene and leave in a warm place until the dough has doubled in bulk. This may take 1 hour.
5. Set the oven to 200°C/400°F/gas mark 6.

6. Divide the dough in two and place on two floured baking sheets. Using the heel of your hand, push and punch the dough into two ovals about 15cm/6 inches in diameter. Leave to rise under greased polythene until one and a half times their original size.
7. When ready, use a sharp knife to score parallel lines in the bread. Brush over the remaining oil, sprinkle with the coarse sea salt, if using, and bake for 15 minutes. Three minutes before the end of the baking time, reheat the garlic cloves in the oven.
8. When the bread and garlic come out of the oven, peel the garlic, crush the flesh and smear over the outside of the loaf or over individual slices.

MELBA TOAST

MAKES 12

PER PORTION Energy: 148kj/35kcal
Fat: 0.3g Saturated fat: 0.1g

6 slices white bread

1. Light the grill and set the oven to
150°C/300°F/gas mark 2.
2. Grill the bread on both sides until
well browned.
3. While still hot, quickly cut off the
crusts and split the bread in half
horizontally.
4. Put the toast in the oven and leave
until dry and brittle.

NOTE: Melba toast can be kept for a
day or two in an airlight tin but it will
lose its flavour if kept longer. It is
undoubtedly best served straight from
the oven.

GRISSINI

This recipe has been taken from
Arabella Boxer's *Mediterranean
Cookbook* (Dent, London, 1981).

MAKES 20

PER GRISSINI Energy: 275kj/66kcal
Fat: 2.6g Saturated fat: 0.4g

7g/½oz fresh yeast
2 teaspoons sugar

3 tablespoons warm water
150ml/¼ pint boiling water
225g/8oz strong flour
1 tablespoon olive oil
1 egg, beaten
55g/2oz sesame seeds

1. Set the oven to 150°C/300°F/gas
mark 2.
2. Dissolve the yeast and sugar in the
lukewarm water.
3. Dissolve the sea salt in the boiling
water, allow to cool to blood
temperature, then mix with the yeast.
4. Sift the flour into a large bowl, make
a well in the centre, pour in the yeast
mixture and the oil. Mix to a soft
dough.
5. Tip the dough on to a floured board
and knead for 3–4 minutes, until
smooth and elastic. Cover with a damp
cloth and leave for 5 minutes. Knead for
3 minutes, then divide into 20 equal
pieces.
6. Roll out each piece of dough until it
is as thick as your little finger. Place on
oiled baking sheets and allow to rise
again for 10–15 minutes.
7. Brush with beaten egg, sprinkle with
sesame seeds and bake for about 45
minutes until crisp and golden brown.

MENU IDEAS

SPRING FORMAL LUNCH OR DINNER PARTY
Menu 1
Sardine and Butterbean Salad *page 92*
Stir-fried Beef in Japanese-style Ginger and Orange Glaze *page 138*
Strawberry and Rosemary Sorbet *page 213*

Menu 2
White Fish Rostis with Salsa Verde *page 93*
Chinese-style Lamb with Mushrooms and Smoked Oysters *page 140*
Bananas Baked with Orange, Lychee and Ginger *page 206*

Menu 3
Spicy Prawns *page 96*
Pasta with Mushrooms and Ginger Sauce *page 175*
Steamed Fruit Parcels *page 203*

Menu 4
Chicken and Spring Vegetable Broth *page 65*
Black and White Pasta with Prawns *page 176*
Rhubarb and Orange Terrine *page 218*

SUMMER LUNCH
Menu 5
Spicy Prawn and Squid Tapas *page 95*
Sauté of Chicken with Nectarines and Chilli *page 118*
Summer Fruits with White Cheese *page 225*

Menu 6
Mediterranean Toasts *page 70*
Salmon with Orange and Ginger *page 108*
Figs and Nectarines in Wine with Raspberries *page 207*

Menu 7
Sauté of Monkfish with Peas and Lettuce *page 94*
Chicken Liver and Mushroom Salad with Pecan Nuts *page 77*
Semi-frozen Red Fruits *page 217*

Menu 8
Fresh Asparagus Dip *page 82*
Chinese Chicken Skewers with Pak-choi *page 117*
Strawberry, Raspberry and Cardamom Granita *page 216*

SUMMER DINNER PARTY
Menu 9
Yakitori-style Skewers *page 75*
Sole Baked in Sauternes with Fennel and Lovage *page 104*
Baked Exotic Fruits *page 205*

Menu 10
Asparagus and Dill in Jelly *page 73*
Honey-roast Sea Bass with Pickled Ginger *page 106*
Gooseberry and Elderflower Sorbet *page 214*

Menu 11
Tomato Sorbet and Avocado Pear Ice *pages 71 & 72*
Citrus-roast Poussin *page 123*
Grilled Peaches with Butterscotch and Whisky Sauce *page 208*

SUMMER INFORMAL DINNER
Menu 12
Baked Bulbs of Garlic or Potato and Garlic Soup *pages 72 & 59*
Spaghetti with Mussels *page 177*
Elderflower and Yoghurt Jelly *page 219*

AUTUMN INFORMAL LUNCH
Menu 13
Yellow Pepper, Onion and Barley Soup
page 63
Spicy Chicken *page 122*
Plums and Vine Fruits with Vanilla *page 267*
Menu 14
Caramelized Parsnip, Apple and Pecan Nut
Soup *page 60*
Morrocan Lamb *page 143*
Grilled Pineapple and Mango Skewers *page 206*

AUTUMN DINNER PARTY
Menu 15
Field Mushroom Pâté *page 81*
Chicken with Prunes, Olives and Capers
page 121
Pear and Orange Pudding *page 224*
Menu 16
Grilled Aubergine with Chick Pea Paste
page 69
Beef Dhansak *page 137*
Spiced Steamed Pears with Grape Sauce
page 204
Menu 17
Sweet and Sour Ceviche *page 91*
Sautéd Lapsang Chicken with Pears and
Shallots *page 119*
Honey and Rosemary Parfait *page 215*
Menu 18
Beetroot and Ginger Soup *page 62*
Pot-roast Lemon Guinea Fowl with Chick
Peas, Courgettes and Sun-dried
Tomatoes *page 126*
Passion-fruit and Mango Jelly *page 220*

WINTER LUNCH OR DINNER PARTY
Menu 19
Lime-marinated Salmon with Papaya *page 90*
Pork and Pumpkin Strudel *page 146*
Grape Jelly with Melon and Plums *page 221*
Menu 20
Chicken Liver and Shiitake Mushroom
Salad *page 77*
Indonesian Fish Curry *page 102*
Baked Apples with Mango and Blueberries
page 205
Menu 21
Leek and Artichoke Mousse *page 74*
Trout with Coriander and Mint Relish *page 107*
Apricot Strudel *page 209*
Menu 22
Prawn Salad Tiède *page 97*
Chicken Lasagne with Red Pepper Sauce
page 124
Citrus and Cranberry Fruit Salad *page 226*
Menu 23
Lentil, Tomato and Lemon Soup *page 64*
Lamb Casserole with Gremolata *page 141*
Striped Fruit Purée Jelly *page 222*

VEGETARIAN LUNCH OR DINNER PARTY
Menu 24
Celeriac and Sun-dried Tomato Dip *page 83*
Mushroom or Radicchio Risotto *pages 180 & 179*
Apple Jelly with Green Fruits *page 221*
Menu 25
Tomato and Red Pepper Soup *page 61*
Spinach Pie *page 168*
Pears in Cider *page 204*

INDEX